ESSENTIAL LIFE SKILLS FOR TEENS

EVERYTHING YOU NEED TO KNOW TO THRIVE IN YOUR TEENAGE YEARS AND BEYOND - LEARN TO CONNECT, COMMUNICATE AND EXCEL AT ALMOST ANYTHING

Emma Davis

Impact
PUBLISHING

© Copyright Impact Publishing, LLC 2024 - All rights reserved. The content within this book may not be reproduced, duplicated, or transmitted without direct written permission from the author or the publisher.

Under no circumstances will any blame or legal responsibility be held against the publisher or author for any damages, reparation, or monetary loss due to the information contained within this book. Either directly or indirectly. You are responsible for your own choices, actions, and results.

Legal Notice:

This book is copyright-protected. This book is only for personal use. You cannot amend, distribute, sell, use, quote, or paraphrase any part of this book's without the author's or publisher's consent.

Disclaimer Notice:

Please note the information contained within this document is for educational and entertainment purposes only. All effort has been expended to present accurate, up-to-date, reliable, and complete information. No warranties of any kind are declared or implied. Readers acknowledge that the author is not engaging in rendering legal, financial, medical, or professional advice. The content within this book has been derived from various sources. Please consult a licensed professional before attempting any techniques outlined in this book.

By reading this document, the reader agrees that under no circumstances is the author responsible for any losses, direct or indirect, which are incurred as a result of the use of the information contained within this document, including, but not limited to, — errors, omissions, or inaccuracies.

TABLE OF CONTENT

Introduction . . . . *V*

Chapter 1	Mastering Money Management 1
Chapter 2	Navigating the Job Market 13
Chapter 3	Communication Skills for Success 25
Chapter 4	Building and Improving Relatiohips 36
Chapter 5	Developing Social Skills 47
Chapter 6	Time Management and Organization 57
Chapter 7	Problem-Solving And Critical Thinking 69
Chapter 8	Personal Health and Wellness 82
Chapter 9	Practical Life Skills 97
Chapter 10	Preparing for the Future 109

Conclusion *125*

About The Author *129*

References *132*

This page has been intentionally left blank

INTRODUCTION

"Skills are the keys that unlock the doors of opportunity, empowering the youth to shape their destiny."

- Anonymous

ARE YOU STRUGGLING to keep up with your pocket money every month? Are you also broke 15 days into the new month? Does your introverted nature keep you from finding a job to sustain personal expenses? Well, this was me as a teenager, and there are high chances that this is you right now. But I suffered so you don't have to, and I bring this guide to you to help you find a path to follow toward becoming a successful person.

Learning skills at a young age is of paramount significance because it sets the foundation for a prosperous life. These skills enable you to develop intellectually and set grounds for personal growth and future opportunities. You, a youngster today, are a leader of tomorrow. So, it is very important to prepare yourself and learn the golden principles of life beforehand.

You wouldn't believe how naïve I was if I were to disclose my experiences as a teenager. I was awful when it came to saving and managing money. I remember when I was 17 years old, I took my father's credit card one day and went to a nearby 7-Eleven to get groceries. I ended up buying up to $2,000 worth of chocolates instead. When my dad came to know of this, he was furious because this impacted the credit score he had meticulously maintained for a long time. But I was a free spirit. To me, expenditures like these never mattered, especially since they weren't my money. Instead, I believed in living in the moment and discouraged the concepts of savings and cutting off expenses for the future. I thought we just lived once and wanted it for me to be king-size.

If only I had any idea that life doesn't work like that. For people belonging to the working class, it is a matter of sustenance. If we don't save money in a timely manner and control how we spend, we might have nothing left when an emergency or uncertainty happens. I learned this lesson the hard way.

During my teenage years, I sought guidance to overcome what I was going through. I was confused and often found myself short of money. Now that I look back on those days, I realize those were some of the most pivotal days of human life. They are consumed with uncertainty and vulnerability. But for me, that time is long gone. However, you must be experiencing this now, which is why you're here.

The said few years are regarded as essential for personal growth, shaping one's character, and setting the groundwork for future endeavors. This is when your mind is most receptive to the new information as your brain is at its peak and capable of forming new neural connections rapidly. Thus, it is an ideal time for learning and acquiring skills that will prepare you for life and provide assistance in areas such as managing money, searching for jobs, enhancing communication skills, working on developing bonds, and consequently becoming successful.

I will be very honest and not hide the fact that at this age, you may find yourself undergoing immense physical and emotional changes. One may observe a range of feelings, including love, fear, anger, confusion, anxiety, and even depression during this phase.

These may form a boundary around you, preventing you from taking risky steps. You may feel alone, unsupported, and disturbed if you do not develop an acceptable solution. You seek guidance, and failing to receive any can lead to unfavorable decisions.

During my research, I realized that children are naturally curious beings. They seek answers and want to understand the world around them from a very early age. They are raw and can be guided to the right way or misguided very easily. Therefore, I found it essential to shield you and show you a way where you can excel positively.

INTRODUCTION

I believe acquiring skills at a young age lays the groundwork for academic and career success in the coming times. You have started growing up and developing knowledge of worldly affairs, so now you can equip yourself with skills like reading, writing, and mathematics. These are some of the basic skills that are essential for success in any field or profession.

Good grades will be closely correlated with your mastery of these abilities. As you grow older, you can follow your passion and discover interests that excite you! Furthermore, the grass is always greener on the other side, so the younger you are introduced, the more chances you have to identify and discover which ones you like or love to do.

> *"There is no trust more sacred than the one the world holds with children. There is no duty more important than ensuring that their rights are respected, that their welfare is protected, that their lives are free from fear and want, and that they can grow up in peace."*
>
> — **Kofi Annan**

Learning skills at a young age enhances social and emotional development in individuals. Communication skills, teamwork, empathy, and conflict resolution are crucial for fostering meaningful relationships and navigating social interactions successfully. Engaging in group projects, team sports, and community service presents children with valuable opportunities to hone these skills and cultivate a well-rounded character that excels in diverse social settings.

Let me elaborate on this in detail:

I. Communication Skills

Honing these skills will help you do wonders in the coming years. These skills will boost your confidence to infinite levels. When you can express yourself confidently in social, academic, and professional settings, you are likely to pursue more opportunities and be capable of voicing your opinions and effectively advocating for yourself on various occasions. With that, this skill will help foster healthy relationships, be they personal or professional. Effective communication skills are also highly sought by employers across industries. They are on a continuous lookout for prospects who can communicate well. These skills are also valued for efficient leadership. You will be able to lead teams and manage projects because of your ability to communicate and connect with people. These skills are deemed essential in every aspect of life

II. Teamwork

Teamwork will teach you how to successfully work with others to attain a common goal. This skill will help you where conjoined efforts are required to accomplish tasks in a well-organized manner, academically or in the workplace. It will help you learn to face problems with the collective approach and provide avenues for brainstorming and making informed decisions. This skill will allow you to expand your networks, which can greatly influence your personal and professional development. This skill will also strengthen you emotionally. You will learn to manage your emotions effectively and become resilient in adversity. It will cultivate positive relationships based on trust and mutual support. It will help you learn another important trait, which is time management, and achieve your objectives in a timely manner. Moreover, these skills will train you to differentiate workload, allocate resources efficiently, and find a balance in your life.

III. Empathy

> *"Empathy is seeing with the eyes of another, listening with the ears of another, and feeling with the heart of another."*
>
> **- Alfred Adler**

Simply put, empathy is the skill to understand what and how other people feel, see things from their point of view, and imagine oneself in their place.

> *"Before you judge a man, walk a mile in his shoes."*
>
> **- Billy Connolly**

This human emotion has almost disappeared from our lives. It seems as if many people have become selfish, with their lives revolving solely around themselves. They don't even consider what other person may think or feel and move on with their perspective.

This skill will enable you to understand others and emotionally connect with them. This skill is the backbone of all the other skills you learn or will learn with time. If you can empathize with someone, you can communicate with them more effectively. You will equip yourself with better knowledge of their attitude and thus form a bond immediately.

This skill will help you become a great leader who is trustworthy, open, and honest, thus fostering harmony and unity within the team. Being empathic will provide you with support from the people around you professionally and personally.

You can anticipate the other's needs and adapt to changing circumstances. Young people who understand others' perspectives and emotions can innovate solutions that address real-world challenges more constructively.

IV. Conflict Resolution

Possession of this skill helps youngsters build better relationships with their parents, siblings, peers, teachers, and colleagues. This enables you to address disagreements and misunderstandings soundly. Learning conflict management reduces the stress and anxiety that comes with interpersonal disagreements. You learn to communicate your needs and boundaries while being receptive to others' viewpoints, promoting open and honest dialogue. You also develop problem-solving skills and equip yourself with the knowledge to identify underlying issues, explore alternative solutions, and negotiate compromises efficaciously. These abilities are transferable to various contexts, including academic, professional, and personal settings as well. This attitude gives way to another attribute: empathy.

It encourages you to recognize the impact of your actions on others and develop a deeper understanding of diverse viewpoints, fostering empathy and tolerance. This trait of effective conflict resolution is considered a hallmark of strong leadership. With this, you can easily mediate conflicts, inspire collaborations, and promote positive changes, thus contributing to a more harmonious environment.

Disagreements are bound to happen in life, and if you can learn how to handle them peacefully and diplomatically, you'll set yourself up for success as you grow. Whether dealing with friends, school affairs, or workplace issues, knowing how to resolve them is key to happiness and success.

You see how these skills can help you and pave the way for your success in numerous ways. Also, we witnessed that these skills are interdependent, carving ways for other attributes that will support you as the world opens before your eyes. Therefore, I would suggest that the provision of sound surroundings where kids can foster and channel these positive attributes should be made possible by their caregivers if they want them to stay on the right track in life. They must do their best if they want the same for these kids and develop methods to achieve that.

Instead of creating an environment where they feel depressed, anxious, afraid, unconfident, and doubtful of their self-esteem, their caregivers should foster and provide opportunities where they can learn to counter these negative personality traits.

Children are susceptible to negativity. Kids who lack these life-saving attributes often fail to cope with this ever-changing world and struggle to become independent while growing up. They lack decision-making skills and scuffle when assessing risks and solving problems efficiently.

Most of these skills are simultaneously linked to professional life and career. Without them, people may find securing and maintaining employment opportunities difficult. They may also struggle to attain financial stability if they do not know how to manage their money.

They may also not successfully form human bonds and build relationships without proper learning. They might find themselves vulnerable for not being informed of setting personal boundaries, thus being on the verge of exploitation and abuse. They may be unable to adapt and face health-related issues due to not being trained in a timely manner.

Therefore, in this book, I will present tips and tricks that I have learned throughout my life—professionally and personally. I will also discuss different theories and ideas presented by experts and life coaches that will benefit young people.

Along with this, I will shed some light on the issue of helping parents, too. I shall provide explications that clarify how giving children essential life skills enhances their mental well-being and ability to move to meet the challenges that life presents.

> *"The best inheritance a parent can give his children is a few minutes of his time each day."*
>
> **- O. A. Battista**

The home is a child's first school. It is a place where, when given proper attention, a child can internalize the motivation to do wonders in life. The parents' role primarily shapes a child's character and core personality, which they will carry with them for their lives.

I will also shed light on the role of educational institutions in shaping a child's life, articulating how teachers can incorporate tricks with the curriculum to form the great leaders of the coming times.

It's not rocket science, but raising a child and making them a responsible part of society is still tricky. I would support that narrative with case studies to eradicate any confusion in the reader's mind. With that, I will suggest ways to be content in life in terms of jobs, wealth, relationships, and success.

This subject has always interested me. Gathering my experiences, especially my teenage years, I have designed a framework that will help young people and their associated people, such as parents, teachers, friends, relatives, etc., gain sufficient knowledge in that regard.

While growing up, my parents termed me a "problem child." I possessed some traits that they found diverging from the prevailing norms and seemed indifferent to me. I believed in standing out with the crowd and thus had developed my own ways to achieve that. They constantly criticized me and expressed their reservations about my conduct quite often.

I felt that void, for I had no proper guidance available to help me at that moment. I was hesitant to discuss my feelings with my dad because I feared he would not understand and restrict my activities.

I grew up in a setting with limited resources, so I always envied the kids born with a golden spoon. I have always wanted to embrace that lifestyle but made many mistakes in pursuing it.

I should have envisioned a much broader spectrum for myself to compensate for the hardships of my childhood. I must have sought guidance through people and books and should have looked for educated ways to help myself.

Instead, I was affected emotionally as well as mentally by the shortcomings I faced at that early age. Consequently, all that filled me with rage and anger toward society and the people around me.

Now, as I look back at this stage, I realize that my feelings weren't entirely baseless and held some truth. However, it was largely influenced by my perception and how I responded to those circumstances. I have been an unguided missile, navigating life without clear direction or guidance. And who better than me can understand the pain of getting misunderstood and wrongly perceived at a young age?

I want to emphasize the need for adequate guidance for teenagers, even if they feel different from me at various points, and that is what I am going to discuss moving forward.

Through these pages, I aim to explore various complexities and nuances of teenagers that are often overlooked. In the upcoming chapters, readers are invited to join me on this journey, where we will delve into the understanding of a young mind, viewing things from their perspectives. The goal is to provide insights into how mentors and guides can support and empower this important demographic of human life. So, are you ready to come along? Let's embark on the success trajectory together.

CHAPTER 1

Mastering Money Management

"Rule No.1: Never lose money. Rule No.2: Never forget rule No.1."

\- Warren Buffett

FEDERAL RESERVE BOARD'S survey of 2022 on the Economic Well-Being of U.S. Households reported that around 37% of Americans fall short of money enough to cover a $400 emergency expense during that fiscal year. There was an increase of 5% compared with the results of 2021, which was 32%. The situation was alarming as it indicated that every one in four consumers would have to use credit, turn to family, sell assets, or get a loan to cover any unexpected expense moving forward. These numbers

can increase drastically in the coming years if adequate measures aren't implemented.

Controlling expenses and managing your money is a daunting process. Sometimes, it appears to be a maze, and you might feel stuck juggling the decisions of where to spend and where to save. You might want to buy an Xbox but must also pay your tuition. I know how difficult it is to make such compromises.

However, how would you feel if I tell you I have some good news for you? What if I tell you that mastering money management skills sets parameters to guide you through this maze? How does it feel if given a chance to imagine a world where you don't have to worry about your finances, are near to accomplishing your goals, and have successfully made your future secure?

This chapter entails the secrets to the art of mastering financial stability, suggesting ways for budgeting, centering savings, and navigating through the credit and debt complexities. Whether you are trying to attain financial stability or looking for ways to make money harder for you, get on this journey to unlock the principles that transform your stress into empowerment. It might also help you alleviate your feelings of FOMO (Fear Of Missing Out) when you acquire resources for yourself.

I. Understanding Personal Finance

As a teenager, you might not make enough money and struggle to save what you get from your parents. Some of you might be working part-time after school and interested in increasing that small amount to gain bigger profits. I understand; I have been in the same situation at your age. I know how being short of funds at a game store feels.

The first step in this process is to understand personal finance. Simply put, it is managing your money to meet your financial goals. It involves evaluating the money you have or what you earn regularly and saving what you left after you are done with your expenses. A small amount may be left, and if you can save that, you are already a step ahead in attaining financial stability. If not, we will discuss it as we move forward in this chapter.

What is a financial goal?

This question may arise in a lot of your minds. Then, 'How is it achieved?' is the second thing that comes to mind. A financial goal is an objective that you have set for your future. It may be buying a new pair of sneakers, getting the latest gaming console, saving up for college fees, or buying someone a gift for the prom night. These small goals that need money to be accomplished fall into this category.

Personal finance is not a one-and-done deal. It is a lifelong practice. Your financial needs and circumstances will change as you evolve, so re-evaluating these goals every few years and adjusting as needed would be a good approach.

Why personal finance is important?

Personal finance, or financial planning, is another side of the same coin. You must have heard that money makes the world go round, but do you know that if you are not financially stable, you might easily stick in a cycle of stress and uncertainty? You can fall into the same pit if you fail to plan your finances adequately and in a timely manner. Let me now explain through some benefits it provides:

1. It helps you attain the financial goals and objectives that you have set for different times.
2. It makes you financially secure by saving for any unexpected events.
3. It enhances your financial decision-making and enables you to ascertain its consequences.
4. It gives you financial independence and liberty to spend wherever you like.
5. It helps to control spending and save from debt.
6. It involves a thorough examination of your income and expenses.
7. It provides an understanding of your financial circumstances at all times.

How to create a financial plan?

Creating a financial plan is a way forward to your goal. By this, you can track your progress, eradicate any doubt or uncertainty about your decisions, and make necessary adjustments to get control over the obstacles that could hinder your journey.

Following are a few steps to be followed when creating a successful financial plan for yourself:

1. **Calculating net worth:** A clear idea of your net worth is a crucial step before making any plans. You must know what amount you keep for yourself and what you owe to others.
2. **Determining the cash flow:** You must know when and how you will receive any cash, whether pocket money, salary, or gift. You cannot just create a plan when no money comes in.
3. **Build an emergency cash fund:** Depending on your cash flow, allocate an amount for an emergency. When setting financial goals, it is important to plan for unforeseen conditions. This will support you and help you not get completely derailed from your objective.
4. **Debt and expense management:** If you have debt, it's better to get rid of it as soon as possible before planning any new financial goal. With that, practice to cut expenses that are not necessary so that you can add more to your savings.
5. **Planning to invest:** Investing in different schemes can help you successfully execute your plan. It may be a faster way to accomplish this plan but also involves risks. Therefore, I advise you to get assistance from your folks when making any investments.

II. Creating and Sticking to a Budget

Now that you understand personal finance and its importance in attaining stability, let me introduce you to an important factor in money management: budget.

Budgeting is getting a clear idea of your finances, controlling them, and saving money for your goals. The whole idea is to organize your money according to your priorities. A budget can help you to avoid borrowing money to fulfill your needs.

> *"Manage your spending by creating and sticking to a budget."*
>
> *- Alexa Von Tobel*

Now, I will give you time to ask how budgeting helps manage expenses. Nine out of 10 people will confirm that it has helped them in various ways. It's a life-saving skill you can benefit from in the long run.

You may notice how inflation has recently heightened and skyrocketed the costs of basic goods and services. Let me tell you, this will not stop there and will increase with the coming time. Only people who have learned to manage their money will survive this efficiently. Therefore, I would request you to emphasize this and prepare yourself for the difficult times.

How to make a budget

Let us now look at the techniques of how to create an effective budget:

1. **Calculate your income-to-expense ratio:** You must draft a budget if you spend more than you earn or get. Having a clear idea about your expenditures will help you set a plan that will manage everything within what you can afford.
2. **Determine your goals:** Setting goals will help create a more suitable budget. It will also motivate you to look for ways to minimize your non-compulsory spending and save for that particular aim.
3. **Finding the best budgeting method:** There are various ways to design your budget. I will discuss some below:
   - **50/30/20 Budget**—This method will help you divide your income into three buckets: 50% for necessary expenses, 30% for discretionary spending, and 20% for savings and debts, in case you have taken loans. You can also create variations tailored to your situation, like 60/20/20 or 70/20/10.
   - **Reverse Budget** – This is also known as the "Pay yourself first" budget. Here, you can in advance decide what percentage or amount you want to save and put that into savings before doing any expenditures as you receive any money.

- **Zero-Based Budgeting** – This doesn't involve any allocations. Instead, you can track every dollar you have and assign it to categories, like whether you want to keep it as a saving or spend it on something. In my opinion, this is the least effective budgeting method and is useless.
- **Envelope Method** – You might have often seen your elders keeping money in envelopes and labeling it for the cause for which it was being saved. This is an old-school method of determining your need, labeling it on an envelope, and then putting money in it to save for a specific reason.
4. **Testing Your Budget**: Once you have selected a budget method, test it for a month or two. If it's not working, change it and try another method. You must also review it regularly to see if it aligns with your circumstances.

How to stick to your budget

Making a budget plan for yourself is much easier than sticking to that habit. Many people who embark on this journey fail miserably because they are not committed to this habit.

I will not leave you stranded by just telling you techniques for effective budgeting. Instead, I will discuss tips and tricks for sticking to this and continuing it, even for a long time.

Here, I would like to add something about human nature. People most often fail to keep up with the habits they adopt from time to time. Therefore, it is necessary to make a note for you guys to develop persistence within yourself. Fix it so that no matter the situation, you guys will keep up with the good habits you will develop. You will work on it and become a better version of yourself.

Let me now present you with the tricks that will help you stick to your budgeting habit:
a. **Hold yourself accountable:** It serves well whenever you allow yourself to change or adopt anything new. When you foster this feeling, you become answerable to yourself, and it is impossible to lie to yourself. Everyone knows about them; thus, it becomes

hard to deceive oneself. So, while budgeting, when you find it hard to keep up, remember the wishes you can fulfill with the money you save and continue. I guarantee that you will improve and accomplish what you aim for once you start reminding yourself about that regularly.
   b. **Make savings an expense in your budget:** This calls for prioritizing your savings. Enright says, "Leaving savings to 'whatever's leftover' usually results in little to no savings." Hence, I suggest treating savings like an expense—a bill that you have to pay; otherwise, you have to face consequences. When budgeting is given importance like that, it becomes hard not to stick to this habit.
   c. **Pay with cash:** When you habitually pay through cards, you lose the emotional touch connected with tangible currency notes. Therefore, try paying more in cash, as it will encourage you to continue with your budgeting.
   d. **Automate your ways:** If you find it hard to record every instance manually, get any tool that may ease the process. Several apps can be installed on cell phones, and everything can be managed "on the go."

These are some of the tricks that I found could help you stick to the habit of managing your expenses on a determined budget. You are welcome to develop or discover your tricks and keep up with this habit.

III. Smart Saving Strategies for the Future

If you want to save up for the future, "budgeting" is one of the smartest strategies you can develop. Also, it is an acclaimed way to attain financial freedom. When you can manage your expenses over the income you generate, you become one step closer to making yourself financially stable. However, there are some other ways as well. They are as follows:
   1. **Create backup funds:** Life is replete with surprises, and no one can ever foresee what is to come next; therefore, it is advised that you be prepared for any adversity ahead of time. Viewing that

possibility, you must set up a fund to help you recover. Also, you can utilize this fund to cover any unexpected expenses.
2. **Pay off credit cards:** Paying your credit card debt is one way to save for your future. To pay this debt, you should choose an interest rate from lowest to highest and then pay the minimum on all except for your highest debt rate. Use any extra funds to make additional payments for the highest-rate card and free yourself as soon as possible.
3. **Pay off student loans:** As you grow up and step into your professional life, make it your priority to repay the loans you took for education.
4. **Consider your dreams:** Set your goals according to your dreams. Allocate budgets for short-, mid-, and long-term goals, separately prioritizing as needed. This will help you save, gradually attain your goals, and move on to the next.

If all the tips I have listed above do not appear useful now, they may serve you in life as you grow up. When you embrace adulthood, many things become mandatory, and you cannot simply shrug them off. You have to face them; thus, I recommend getting yourself equipped beforehand.

IV. Navigating Credit and Debt Wisely

Now, let me take you on a journey to another realm. This is the aspect that has ruined numerous lives. You may have witnessed people going bankrupt and then becoming homeless consequently. This happened because they could not maintain their credit score and repay their debts on time. I recommend acquiring less debt as possible or a lower interest-rate credit. However, if you took any (which is inevitable, in most cases), I will suggest using it wisely. Here, I am listing down some positive habits that you should pay heed to when managing credit:
1. You should borrow only what you need. I will advise you not to fall for the loan offers that may appear lucrative at first but, under the disguise of their "hidden terms," milk you out well of

your finances. You must also take care that you are not borrowing anything more than you need, for it will become tough repaying the extra for no reason. Be mindful while swiping your credit cards, and keep an eye on their interest rates.
2. You must develop a habit of paying your credit bills in full every month. These cards offer to pay 1 – 3% of your total balance, which is tempting, and several people fall for that. They utterly ignore that they will be charged for the remaining balance, which keeps increasing the longer they are held.
3. Always pay your bills on time. Never ignore your service payments. While your utility company, doctor, or landlord isn't charging interest for late or missed payments, it can badly affect your credit report. If you are past due on payments, you may be contacted by a debt collector, which is very harmful to your credit and is not advisable.
4. It is recommended that you keep the borrowing ratio on your credit card up to 30% of the credit limit (try to keep it even less) and not max it out. Maxing the card can lead you into a debt cycle trap, impose penalties, negatively impact your credit history, cause a drop in credit score, and cause loss of card benefits.

As you grow up, I will ask you to focus on developing healthy habits rather than maintaining good credit scores. You are more than just numbers; it is important to be financially stable. Work on reducing your spending and utilize the free resources available to you.

Hopefully, you have gained enough knowledge to control expenses and prevent financial ruin. It is time to learn effective ways to generate income. This will allow you to steer the wheel of your financial destiny and take full control. Just as a car's direction alters with each turn, human trajectory changes with every career opportunity. So, set your spirits high as I take you to the world of infinite opportunities, guiding you toward the uncharted territories of personal and professional growth.

Key Takeaways

- Financial stability starts when one begins to align their income and expenses accordingly.
- Small goals can help save big for the future.
- Budgeting plays a vital role in gaining financial stability.
- There are different methods of budgeting.
- Budgets must be tested regularly to check if they are being done in the desired manner.
- Dividing your income into parts based on your needs, savings, and miscellaneous expenses can help you reach your goal.
- Aspirations must be considered when setting your financial goals.
- Credit and debts must be managed efficiently.
- Loans must be acquired only when required.
- Credit cards must be paid promptly and fully every month.
- It is better not to use more than 30% of the total credit limit on your card.
- Bills must be paid on time. Once you fall into a debt trap, it becomes difficult to get out of it.

Exercise

To illustrate a hands-on approach to financial planning, we will create a budget specifically for you while considering the money management concepts introduced in this chapter.

Instructions:

1. List all your income sources, from part-time or casual jobs, allowances, or pocket money.
2. Write your basic expenses, such as essentials (daily acquirement of food, transportation, and stationary) and non-essentials (leisure, maybe hobbies, etc.).
3. Divide the expenses into two categories: fixed (paid monthly) and variable (which can change every month).
4. Create your own financial goals that you would like to reach soon with your money, such as a new phone, and in the long run, such as having enough money for college.
5. Divide your income between your expenses and financial goals. First, you must budget money for the necessary items and savings before you can splurge on unnecessary items.
6. Review your budget periodically to know whether you are compliant or how to exceed it and make adjustments. This could be achieved through carefully evaluating your expenditures and considering where cuts could be made or searching for more income.
7. Reflect on your decisions and think about the difference you are making with the money you have. Are you spending money on the stuff that pleases you, or do you tend to spend money on other stuff that doesn't add value to your life? Have there ever been options that you could be using to save?
8. Record your expenses to determine where you might waste your money over time. This way, the plan will stay flexible, and you can constantly adapt to changes.

9. On your journey, celebrating your achievements—reaching a savings target or keeping to your budget for a month—becomes an integral part of what motivates you.
10. Avoid putting a financial matter in the back of your mind without confiding in your parent, tutor, or financial advisor if you need help managing your money or budgeting.

Remember, mastering money management takes time and practice. By creating and sticking to a budget, you're taking an important step toward financial independence and success.

CHAPTER 2

Navigating the Job Market

"I can't change the direction of the wind, but I can adjust my sails to always reach my destination."-

Jimmy Dean

MAN IS FULL of desires, making them work hard to make it big. You put your best foot forward when you eye a target and have a specified goal. However, everything in this world has a price. You cannot just pick from the tree anything you want. You have to earn it, and to get what you want, you need "money."

A job is one of the most respectable ways to earn money. This helps you fulfill your needs, allows you to explore your potential, and brings you one step closer to what you have aimed for.

It is a pretty decent method of attaining financial stability. Yet, getting a job that suits your needs is hard, and not many people often get work that suits their choice. Therefore, in this chapter, I will discuss the problems faced while navigating the job market and present you with techniques for making it effective.

I. Identifying Your Strengths and Interests

Identifying what you want to do is critical for an effective career plan. I consider it a "primary" step in assessing suitable career options for yourself. Understanding your strengths and passions will enable you to make informed decisions. It will also lead you to a professional path where you can pursue a career that will bring satisfaction and fulfillment as you move forward.

Let us now discuss how you can recognize what your skills and strengths are:

1. **Self-assessment:** Take a personal inventory of your skills and interests. Gather your past experiences and reflect on your hobbies and academic achievements. Consider activities that energize you. All these hint at your strengths.
2. **Values and Passions:** Consider your values, beliefs, and passions. Contemplate the ones that are most important to you and your surroundings. This will help you align your career choices with your principles.
3. **Seek Feedback:** Reach out to your family, friends, colleagues, or mentors and take feedback on your skills and interests. They may provide you with insights or observations that you either have missed out on or didn't even consider about yourself.
4. **Career and Strength Assessments:** From time to time, use online assessments to evaluate your skills, interests, and personality traits. Several resources are available on the internet. Take the time to give them a try.
5. **Job Shadowing and Internships:** You can also explore different careers through job shadowing and internships. This will allow you to observe experienced professionals in various fields firsthand. Doing so will help you gain knowledge of the skills needed to be successful. Also, you can determine what careers align with your interests.
6. **Volunteer Work:** You can volunteer and contribute to your community while searching for a job. It will contribute to your skills and direct your interests to meaningful causes. It will also allow you to network. In my opinion, it is an excellent opportunity to broaden your horizons. It helps you gain a new perspective on how life works in the real world.

7. **Professional Development:** Find ways to polish and acquire new skills. Attend workshops and seminars or enroll in online courses. These can help you discover new interests and expand your knowledge in specific areas.
8. **Industry Research:** By the time you look for a job, conduct research on industries, job roles, and career paths that align with skills and interests side by side. You can also utilize career planning services and career development platforms.
9. **Look for Professional Help:** Reach out to professionals in your field of interest. This will allow you to learn about their roles, the skills required, and the day-to-day realities of those careers. Their experience can give you valuable information to help guide you in your professional journey.
10. **Networking:** Build a professional network by connecting with individuals in your field. Gain insights and uncover new interests to grow your career by looking for networking opportunities.

The job-hunting game doesn't come easy and can be overwhelming. A series of failures may dishearten you. However, remember to be strong. Keep pushing forward, stay resilient, and opportunities will come your way. You've got this!

II. Crafting a Winning Resume and Cover Letter

A resume plays an important role in searching for a job. Through that, you introduce yourself, referencing the skills and qualifications that make you suitable (or not) for a specific job role. Simply put, you market yourself through your resume – it's your shop window!

Now, you may ask: **What is the difference between a resume and a cover letter?** It's a valid question. At the start of my career, I struggled with the same issue.

A resume summarizes your work experience, while a cover letter provides why you are the right person for the job. A resume is a document that lists your employment history, summarizing the jobs you have had and the education you attained. It also shows certifications, hard and soft skills, and other information about your background and experience. Many employers only require a resume to be submitted with a job application. A cover letter may not be required. However, including one while applying for a job can increase your chances of getting selected for an interview.

A resume is written in the third person, and as few words as possible are used to summarize your information. It mostly entails one or two pages about your experiences. A cover letter, on the other hand, provides additional information to the employers. It suggests to them why they should hire you. Its main purpose is to show off your qualifications and make you a better match for the particular job.

III. How to Build Your Resume

Let's explore how to create a strong resume that catches the eye of the recruiter and lands you a job. Three types of resumes are chronological, functional, and targeted.

1. **Chronological Resume:** This is the most commonly used resume format. Employers also prefer it because it is easy to scan. If you have never built your resume, chronological resumes are suggested as the best choice. This resume lists your work in order of the date, with your most recent position at the top. Unlike the other two types of resumes, chronological resumes can be sent to multiple employers without the need to be edited every time, as they cover everything.
2. **Functional Resume:** A functional resume highlights work experience and skills rather than specific positions or dates of employment compared to a chronological one. This format is widely used by job seekers switching careers or having gaps in their employment history.
3. **Targeted Resume:** This resume focuses on a specific job opening. It's written to highlight specific skills and experiences relevant

to a particular job opening. This type of resume is edited or rewritten for each job you apply to match the job description.

Job seekers can choose any of the formats above. However, there are certain guidelines that most resumes must follow to gain employers' attention. Here's some information that you must be sure to include while writing a resume:

Identification

You must not forget to include your name, address, contact number, and email address in the topmost section of your resume. I recommend you add a professional email address rather than a funky one. If you don't have one, first get a proper email address and begin with your resume writing.

Objective

This is an optional section; you can choose not to include it in your resume. However, keep it specific and concise if you decide to add it. State your desired job or field and what you aim to accomplish there. Keep it to no more than four or five sentences.

Education

This section cannot be ignored and must be added to a resume. It includes your academic accomplishments that make you a strong candidate for the job. You need to include the following information:
- If you have more than one degree, list them in reverse chronological order (with the most recent degree listed first).
- Be sure to include the name of each educational institution, its location, and the date (or expected date) of your graduation.
- Include your major/minor fields, as well as your GPA and any honors, publications, and projects, if applicable. Otherwise, your resume will get bulky and unappealing.

- Do not include your high school degree unless you are a current high school student.

Experience

This is the most important section of your resume. It aligns you with the specifications of the job posted by the employer. Here's how you should craft it:
- Include your work experiences in reverse chronological order (with the most recent one listed first).
- Include jobs, internships, and voluntary work. High school students might also include clubs and sports.
- Include the name of the company, the position, and dates of employment.
- Roughly list three important tasks, accomplishments, or skills gained at each job. Use action verbs to describe your achievements. Avoid passive phrases such as "responsible for" and "duties include."

Skills

This section is optional and included only when a job seeker has considerable professional skills. If not, you can skip this section. Things to be added in this section are listed below:
- Any computer skills you are proficient in, particularly if they relate to the position you are applying to.
- Any foreign languages with which you are familiar can be added. State both the language and your familiarity level (beginning, intermediate, proficient, or fluent).
- Any other skills you possess related to the job and have not been included anywhere else in the resume.
  - **Hobbies and Interests:**

This is an optional section; you can include it only when needed. Otherwise, it is irrelevant and should be avoided. If you apply to work at a sports store, you can add your passion for basketball; if not, leave it.

Note:

- Remember to keep your resume as concise as possible. The typical maximum length recommended is two pages, but one page is preferable if you can fit your information on a single page.
- Don't add personal information such as birth date, height, weight, social security number, marital status, children, etc., on your resume. It's irrelevant and not required.

How to Write a Cover Letter

Just as a resume enables you to highlight your work-related experience, skills, and achievements, the cover letter implies the value of your draw to the hiring firm. It will let them bridge what the company wants and what you have to offer.

The trick to writing a cover letter is not much different than resume writing. You just need to be detailed and descriptive about how you can be a valuable addition to the company. The body of your cover letter tells the employer the position you are applying for, why you should be called for an interview, and how you will follow up.

Then, highlight examples of your work and the results you accomplished during your professional journey. If you are applying for your first job, highlight your educational background, skills, and qualities in a very crisp manner. Share your knowledge of the company and how you can contribute to its growth. Finally, close your letter by suggesting a meeting.

Resumes and cover letters alone won't get you a job. They'll help you win an interview, and then it's upon your luck and skills how you ace that. I have presented comprehensive information to guide you through writing a targeted resume and cover letter. With that, I believe you can begin your search for a great. Next, I will discuss the techniques required for effective job searching.

IV. Effective Job Searching Techniques

Securing a job is never easy. With the influence of technology over various industries and job requirements, it has become even more challenging. This scenario serves as a wake-up call for job seekers to reshape their strategies to stand out and increase their chances of success.

I am going to discuss some of the techniques below that I find reliable to navigate the challenges of the job market that have gotten fast-paced and extremely competitive:

1. **Online Presence:** A powerful online presence will give you a considerable edge in job prospects in today's technology-driven world. You must make sure that you have a LinkedIn profile that tells your professional story, reflects your abilities, and demonstrates your skills. You need to take your efforts a level higher by optimizing your profile using the most relevant keywords that will help you when recruiters are searching for potential candidates. Additionally, you can build a website to showcase your work, projects, and accomplishments. These can serve as your online portfolios that can be accessed from anywhere. This will give the recruiter a comprehensive overview of your capabilities, increasing your chances of getting an interview.
2. **Remote Work:** Remote work has risen significantly since the COVID-19 pandemic. Their geographical limitations no longer bind candidates; they can explore opportunities globally. People working remotely have a great work-life balance, which has made it attractive to job seekers. You can leverage this trend, search for jobs, and mention your remote work capabilities in your applications.
3. **Learning and Upskilling:** You must remember that the job market is continuously evolving. With that, employers seek people who are adaptable and willing to learn. Your current skills and education are insufficient to help you get a job. Therefore, keep on learning and upskilling yourself. It will enhance your qualifications and demonstrate your proactive attitude toward

personal and professional growth. And this is what employers are looking for.
4. **Networking:** Networking is one of the most powerful tools in the job search. You should attend networking events, join professional organizations, and participate in online communities to build strong connections. Through networking, you can interact with industry professionals, gain insights into potential job openings, and receive referrals to increase your job prospects.
5. **Utilizing Job Search Platforms:** Job search platforms have completely transformed how candidates search for jobs. These platforms, powered by AI, provide personalized recommendations based on candidates' skills and preferences. It saves a lot of time and effort in the job search process.
6. **Crafting Cover Letters:** While some cover letters may seem a mere formality, they can make you stand out as a candidate. A well-crafted and personalized cover letter can increase your chances of being noticed by prospective employers.
7. **Building a Portfolio:** A portfolio is a powerful asset for tech industry candidates. It allows them to showcase their work, projects, and accomplishments and is tangible evidence of their skills and expertise.
8. **Soft Skills and Emotional Intelligence:** Besides technical skills, you should also focus on learning soft skills and emotional intelligence. These include communication, adaptability, problem-solving, etc. Employers value these skills and seek out candidates who are proficient in them.

Remember, if you do not keep up with the pace of this ever-changing world, you will fall behind personally and professionally. Nowadays, securing a job requires a multifaceted approach. Using the aforementioned techniques can improve your chances of landing a rewarding job. Keep your spirits high, and do not get upset by the initial setbacks.

V. Acing Interviews and Following Up

Once you get a call for an interview, you need to work on making a good impression on the interviewer. It can be nerve-wracking, but by adequate preparation, you can better convince the employer that you are the best choice for the job.

What should you do when going to an interview? Here are some tips:

- **Learn about the company:** The first step is to research the. Conduct thorough research by visiting the company's website. Your knowledge about the company can impress hiring managers and increase your chances of getting hired.
- **Be on time:** Whenever you are called for an interview, remember to be on time. It's best to be there 10 - 15 minutes before your interview time. This will give you time to take some deep breaths to calm yourself and give the employer an impression of your timeliness.
- **Prepare in advance:** Prepare yourself before going to the interview. Research some commonly asked interview questions and gather answers, such as, "Tell us about yourself" or "Where do you see yourself in five years?"
- **Review the job posting:** Go through the job description and details again before you go to the interview. It will be helpful if you interview for multiple positions so you don't mix them up.
- **Prepare your questions:** Make a list of questions you want to ask the interviewer. This will help you address your concerns or clear any confusion regarding the job or the company. When they ask if you have any questions, always ask one or two to show your interest in the position.
- **Engage in a conversation:** Start a conversation with your interviewer. This dialogue will help determine whether you, the organization, and the job are well-matched.
- **Dress appropriately:** Dress professionally when going to an interview. Make sure you are groomed appropriately. It will make a good first impression.

- **Take your resume:** Bring copies of your resume to the interview. Also, take a small notepad and pen to write down notable things, such as concluding how well you did. This will help you perform better in the next round of interviews.
- **Listen carefully:** Pay attention to what the interviewer is asking. Listen carefully and then answer the question completely. If you don't understand anything, ask for clarification. Stick to the point and answer concisely.

Remember that you may not land a job after the first interview and can be called for more interview rounds. Stay positive and confident during your interview. Greet the interviewer before and after the meeting and maintain eye contact throughout.

The tips and tricks mentioned in this chapter can help you get a job and start your professional career. If not, they will prepare you for the long run, as these techniques may become useful in various phases of life. Next, we are going to talk about communication and how to communicate well. So, come along as we continue on this journey of learning skills that are essential for job hunting.

Key Takeaways

- Working is one of the most decent ways to earn money.
- Jobs help attain financial stability and provide a chance for personal growth and development.
- Strengths and interests must be identified before looking for a job.
- You should consider your values while looking for a job.
- A resume and cover letter are essential for your job search.
- An effective cover letter may allow you to stand out before the hiring manager.
- You should have a strong online presence on professional sites like LinkedIn.
- You should be ready to adhere to the ever-changing standards of the modern world.

- Prepare yourself before going for an interview.

> **Summary of actionable steps:**
>
> - Be adaptive and flexible.
> - Keep learning and acquiring new skills.
> - Keep up with technological changes.
> - Seek feedback and look for ways to improve.
> - Build a strong and dependable network.
> - Identify your goals and objectives.
> - Consider volunteer work to meet more people.
> - Learn soft skills and enhance emotional intelligence.

CHAPTER 3

Communication Skills for Success

"If you just communicate, you can get by. But if you communicate skillfully, you can work miracles."
- Jim Rohn

ONE ATTRIBUTE THAT most people lack is "communication," or, let's rephrase it, "effective communication." I have found that such people do not realize what they lack; hence, they never work toward improving that aspect.

It's a two-way road. You must learn to listen first and then reciprocate accordingly. This is called "active listening." When you listen to what is being said, you can better understand what you are required or supposed to do in response.

Only listening is not enough. You must also learn how to reply and engage in meaningful conversations. People don't realize that and talk meaninglessly without proper closures. They must ensure that what they say is comprehendible and delivered as required.

Communication serves as a foundation for shaping our actions in society. It helps humans connect, develop bonds, and work together for one another's betterment. Therefore, in this chapter, we will learn about communication concepts and how they can be effectively incorporated into our lives.

I. The Art of Verbal and Non-Verbal Communication

Communication is the art of interaction and exchanging ideas with the people around you. It is an innate aspect of human disposition, and no one can deny its importance. Whether you speak, communicate a message to another party, or share information. The entire communication process occurs between two parties: (a) the Sender and (b) the Receiver.

Primarily, communication is classified into two types:
1. Verbal
2. Non-Verbal

Verbal Communication

This takes place when you converse using "words" to exchange information. This can be either in the form of speech or writing. It is supposed to be one effective means of communication that leads to a rapid interchange of facts and feedback. There are fewer chances of misunderstanding as the conversation between the parties is clear as the words are involved during the exchange.

Communication can be done orally, like face-to-face conversation, lectures, phone calls, seminars, etc., or you can write what you want to say in letters, text messages, emails, etc. However, this communication can be further divided into the following two types:

- **Formal Communication:** It is also called official communication. This occurs by following a proper and pre-defined channel for exchanging information between both parties, i.e., sender and receiver. Here, the flow of information is controlled, and deliberate effort is required to communicate properly. This includes business letters, sales reports, purchase orders, etc.
- **Informal Communication:** It is most commonly termed "grapevine." It occurs when the sender and receiver do not follow pre-defined channels. It can be a conversation at a family dinner table, interactions between friends and colleagues, or in any setting that is not "formal."

Non-Verbal Communication

When communication occurs between two parties without any words and by merely understanding each other, it is called non-verbal communication.

This form of communication uses various signs and signals. The communication is deemed successful if the receiver deciphers the message the sender conveys through any of these mediums and provides proper feedback.

It also compliments verbal communication many times. It helps both parties understand the mindset and status, which is not spoken but understood through body language and gestures.

The types of non-verbal communication are as follows:
- **Chronemics:** The involvement of time while communicating is called chronemics. This indicates either party's personality, such as punctuality, speed of speech, etc.
- **Vocalics:** The volume, tone of voice, and pitch used to interchange information with the speaker is known as vocalics or paralanguage.
- **Haptics:** The use of touch in communication is considered an expression of feelings and emotions between both parties involved.
- **Kinesics:** The study of a person's body language, i.e., gestures, postures, facial expressions, etc., is called kinesics.
- **Proxemics:** How close people stand when they talk can show how they feel about each other. It tells whether they are close and friendly or more distant and formal.
- **Artifacts:** A person's appearance reflects their personality traits and says a lot about them by how they dress, carry jewelry, observe their lifestyle, etc. This type of communication is called artifactual communication.

Verbal and non-verbal communication go side by side. They both complement one another. As someone has rightly said, "Actions speak louder than words." Therefore, your body language must not signal otherwise with what you are saying to avoid any misinterpretations. People are quick to judge your physical expressions, and if they get the gist of your lack of interest, they might leave the conversation and go away.

II. Listening Skills and Empathy in Conversations

You may have noticed that while talking to someone, you have to wait for them to stop so that you can say what you want. You cannot just interfere and put your point there. This is something that is considered "indecent" about human attributes. You also might expect them to listen to you completely tuned into your words.

This is a commonly observed attitude in our society that shows a lack of active listening, as people only think about their responses and do not pay attention to what the other person is talking about.

Communication is only fruitful if it involves active listening and empathy. Otherwise, it is just a bunch of words wasted by not putting to a proper usage. Active listening involves eye contact and an amalgamation of verbal and non-verbal communication. This includes bodily features, such as nodding the head, responding aptly, and asking questions for added clarifications. Empathy means understanding and caring about how someone else feels or thinks and showing that you relate to them. This combination of active listening and empathy is called "empathetic listening" and has been pivotal in improving relationships, from couples and families to friends and coworkers.

A question may arise regarding how to hone these empathetic listening skills. Worry not; I have done thorough research on the subject. Let me share my findings here.

Empathetic Listening Skills

1. For empathic listening, you must listen patiently to what the other has to say. It doesn't matter if you agree; just listen carefully first. Do not jump the gun and do slight nodding. It's better to use small phrases like "I see" or "I understand" without disrupting the flow of the conversation.

2. Sense what the speaker is feeling or trying to do. Always be conscious of the emotional aspect of the content while referring to the literal meaning of the words delivered as well.
3. Stand in front of the mirror and practice that. Imagine someone is talking to you. Stay calm, and try to resonate with them. Feel what they are going through. If you were in their place, how would you have reacted?
4. While talking to someone, give them your undivided attention, even if the interaction is brief. Remove any distractions, like putting your phone away. Maintain eye contact throughout.
5. Sometimes, you don't even need to say anything. People just want to be heard, and you can provide them with an avenue by making them available.
6. If someone pauses, judge the context and the quality of the silence before responding. The person might think about what to say next or need a moment to rein in any emotions.
7. If you choose to speak, refer to the person's condition, ask questions, and clarify comments as needed. Keep that non-judgmental approach and give them a moment to respond.
8. Pay attention to what is not being said. Try to read between the lines and try to comfort them.

Keep in mind that there is no fixed script or manual for empathetic listening. It is based on responses, depending on the situation and the moment involved during the conversation. It is something you learn from real-life experiences and interactions.

Overcoming Communication Barriers

You might have been involved in conversations but didn't get the response you sought, or you were perceived wrongly against what you wanted to convey. This happens when communication barriers exist that may hinder effective communication.

Types of Communication Barriers

Yes, some obstacles might come in the way and make people understand you; otherwise, they may create a negative persona. I know this is a harsh statement, but this is ultimately what happens.

1. **Verbal Barriers:** You may be very good at your language and have a grip over a vast set of vocabulary. Or you may have a nice, polite way of talking, but if your choice of words is incorrect, you may find it difficult to deliver what you want. The same goes for the tone and the structure of the sentence you utilize.
2. **Language Barriers:** It's obvious that if you are unfamiliar with any language, you will find it difficult to converse efficiently. When two people don't speak the same language, getting on the same page makes it difficult for them. Additionally, every language has its dialect, syntax, and morphology. While communicating in another language, these aspects may influence the entire conversation, and others may find it hard to decipher the actual message.
3. **Lack of Clarity and Conciseness:** You can never communicate effectively if you don't speak clearly. Complicated sentences and difficult words can confuse listeners about what you are trying to say.
4. **Use of Jargon and Technical Terms:** If you are associated with some specific industry and habitual of using related technical terms and jargon in your day-to-day conversation, you may find it hard to communicate. This will work fine if your receiver belongs to the same field as you, but others cannot relate to that, and you will fail to get the desired output.
5. **Nonverbal Barriers:** We often ignore our nonverbal cues, which can alter our conversation. If used wisely, these can complement our words. Otherwise, they can be a major barrier to communication. These can be our body language, gestures, facial expressions, eye contact, etc.
6. **Distance and Physical Space:** It becomes hard to communicate effectively if you are talking to someone unavailable in a space

similar to yours. For example, if you are talking to a person in another room, there's a possibility they are standing out of earshot and cannot hear you properly. On the other hand, you are speaking with all your efforts to deliver the message, but the proximity between you is acting as an obstacle. Similar is the case if you're too close. Firstly, it's a very awkward position to talk. Secondly, either that person has to lean way, maintaining a distance, or he or she will walk away, leaving you stranded over there.

7. **Written Barriers:** Written communication is equally important as verbal communication. Whether emails, text messages, or social media posts, words are used in writing to share thoughts, feelings, and important messages. With that, people visit news sites, review products, and read blogs. However, if there are typos, incorrect use of grammar, and spelling mistakes, no matter how attractive these writing pieces are, they fail to garner the reader's attention and get the desired outcome.

8. **Cultural Barriers:** It also sometimes becomes difficult to communicate with people from a diffcrent culture. There is a sheer possibility that even a simple gesture can be misinterpreted while interacting with foreign people.

These are some of the barriers that may trouble you while achieving the target of effective communication. You need to be very attentive while getting involved in conversations with people.

You must now think that communicating requires much effort to be effective. No, it's not like that. In fact, it is very easy, and you are already doing that. Mentioning and talking about things in detail gives you a different perspective on how you can interact daily. Like all the previous skills we have discussed, it will also help you through the different phases of life. You just need to put that all into practice, and you will notice improvement very soon.

III. Digital Communication in the Modern World

This is the 21st century, and we can witness the digital revolution all around us. Everything in this world is now digitized, affecting how we communicate. It is visible from the past that communication has always been in the process of evolution. Our ancestors' methods are entirely different from those we are using. Every time, there has been a shift, and the chances of getting the means of communication influenced by that have always been inevitable.

The world has now become a global village, and everyone has the power to communicate globally. The advent of technology has made it possible for individuals to connect and collaborate in the broader societal contexts within the country and across boundaries using modern ways of communication for social interactions.

Let us now view the forms of digital communication we are using in our daily lives:

Audio Communication

It is one of the oldest means of communication that has evolved with time. We could only make calls earlier, but now we can send recorded messages. We can record our calls and conduct numerous personal and professional tasks.

Text-Based Communication

Emails and instant messaging have enabled us to conduct real-time text-based conversations. They have shortened the distance, and we can connect with anyone, regardless of location. We would write letters in the past, but reaching their destination would take quite a while. Additionally, they allow us to send emotions as Emojis and GIFs, adding a sentimental dimension to our text messages.

Visual Communication

It has provided us access to watch and share visual content, conveying complex ideas in a simplified manner. Memes, in this aspect, have become a cultural phenomenon. It has revolutionized personal and professional communication through video calls, which are now used as a common method of communication.

Social Media

Social media is a blend of text, image, and video-based communication. It also provides a platform for entertainment. It gives access to democratized freedom of expression and efficiently conveys our thoughts and ideas. As a modern-age interaction tool, it is also used for major business activities. It has become a marketplace for common commercial activities.

A large number of people are using various social media platforms nowadays. No one denies their importance in these times, but using them properly is still left undiscussed. Since many young people are there, I feel an urge to discuss the etiquette they should observe while using them.

Etiquettes to Be Followed on Social Media

Privacy: In your online interactions, take the necessary measures to ensure your privacy. Privacy in communication is critical as it promotes trust and creates a healthy digital environment. While it is okay to share information online, avoiding spreading sensitive information without consent is equally important. You must also have an avid understanding of your platforms' privacy policies.

Appropriate language: Always make sure you are using proper language on social media. People here are instigated and might get offensive, using foul language. Make sure you act otherwise. Even if someone offends you, stay calm; if you can't handle it, sign off for a while. Give it a thought and come back when you are relaxed and composed.

Online respect: Maintain the level of respect here as well. People here are no different, irrespective of where they belong. You must try to give equal respect to everyone online. Cultivating respectful digital interactions will help you gain a wide audience on social media platforms.

Positive impression: Your actions define your personality. This same works in the digital world as well. The way you present yourself determines how you are being perceived online. Your positive digital body language can enhance your online image and persona.

Mindful of tone: Be cautious while setting your tone online. After you type something, take a moment and review your words. Adjust the tone by considering how your message will be perceived. Use Emojis wisely.

The manners you must maintain in the digital world are no different than those of the real world. So, what you follow in your house, at your school, and how you treat your parents, siblings, and friends should also be what you practice in your online interactions. It's the same world, consisting of the same beings as you witness around, but in a digital realm.

By now, you must have understood how to foster good communication standards, whether offline or online. In the coming chapter, we will discuss how to work on your existing relationships, especially cultivating new ones. We, humans, cannot survive alone. We need someone to take care of us as well as someone to be taken care of.

Key Takeaways

- Communication is a two-way thing.
- You need to listen before you can respond.
- There are two types of communication: verbal and non-verbal.
- Verbal communication can be done via text or speech.
- Your actions define your personality.
- Listening and empathy together form empathetic or empathic listening.
- You need to listen patiently to understand the other person's feelings.
- You must refer to the emotional aspect of the content before reciprocating.
- While in conversation, give undivided attention to the speaker.
- Take time and figure out the barriers that hinder your path to effective communication.
- Social media is not a realm to loaf around.
- You need to be extra cautious and take care of your overall impression in the digital world.

Summary of actionable steps:

- Be respectful in your conversations, online or offline.
- Be mindful of the language you use in your interactions.
- Listen actively.
- Provide proper feedback.
- Think twice before you speak.
- Be clear and concise in your conversations.
- Don't get too technical.
- Learn email communication manners.
- Observe the same demeanor on social media as in real life.

CHAPTER 4

Building and Improving Relatiohips

"Develop an intentional relationship building with people that matter in your life. Never be casual about your relationships except the relationships that add no value to your life."

- Benjamin Suulola

HUMANS ARE SOCIAL animals. Our neurological systems are designed in a way that needs the company of other people around us. We cannot live in isolation. Though some people might be introverted, they also need others around them to survive from time to time in their lives. It is nearly impossible for someone to live alone in this world.

It is observed that relationships make people happy and satisfied with their lives. As a result, they are less likely to have any physical and mental problems.

Therefore, you are encouraged to develop healthy relationships as you move forward in life. Now, how would you do that, and what are the steps involved in that process? That is what we are going to discuss in this chapter. But first, here are the different types of relationships and their significance in our lives.

I. Understanding Different Types of Relationships

We meet different people in our lives. Several behavioral patterns are involved as we relate, interact, and communicate with them. These patterns are called relationship dynamics. These dynamics shape and affect our overall relationships. However, awareness and understanding of these dynamics put us in control, enabling us to navigate the challenges we face during our interactions in the world.

There are many different types of relationship dynamics, but here we will discuss some of the common ones that revolve around the nature of relationship itself:

Romantic dynamics: Emotional intimacy, love, and often sexual components are included in these dynamics. The relationships around these dynamics range from mere infatuations to long-term partnerships and marriages.

Platonic dynamics: This type of bond is shared between friends. Mutual trust, shared interests, and emotional support characterize human friendships. These friendships can be of different levels depending on the closeness and intimacy between friends. It does not involve any physical intimacy.

Familial dynamics: Humans sharing the same bloodline or who have come closer because of some legal arrangements share these dynamics. These include relationships between parents and children, siblings, and extended family members.

Professional dynamics: These dynamics are observed when people share interests in a professional environment, like while in a job or doing some business. These include relationships with colleagues, managers, employees, or business partners.

Casual dynamics: When people are not serious in their relationships, these dynamics provide a reason for that. They show a low level of commitment and invest minimally in emotions and sentiments. Relationships that involve such dynamics include casual dating, hookups, and friendships with fewer emotional connections.

Toxic dynamics: These dynamics are unhealthy and give rise to a relationship that can be abusive, physically as well as emotionally. These can occur in any context of human life, including romantic, sexual, financial, familial, or friendships.

Codependent dynamics: These dynamics entail dependence on one person over another for emotional support or self-esteem. If you look closely, such relations can be unhealthy and impede the process of self-growth.

Long-distance dynamics: These dynamics involve partners who live far apart and maintain their relationship via communication and occasional visits.

Open or polyamorous dynamics: These dynamics occur when partners mutually agree on non-monogamous arrangements, allowing each other to have multiple romantic or sexual partners. Now, how positive the relationship develops in this setting is debatable.

Mentorship or teacher-student dynamics: These include the bond that is shared between people who seek guidance and enlightenment for personal and professional growth.

Online dynamics: These dynamics occur when people connect digitally through social media, online gaming, or dating apps.

Parent-child dynamics can be termed the purest and most honest bond humans form during their lives. These dynamics play a vital role in a child's development and shape his/her overall personality.

Every human relation is subjected to any one of these dynamics. These dynamics have both positive and negative impacts on their lives. The healthier these dynamics are, the easier it gets to foster a healthier relationship.

Role of Trust and Respect

Trust and respect are the most important aspects of building a healthy relationship. No good relationship can be attained if any of these are missed. Your relationship can become strained and eventually crumble if you fail to observe these.

Trust provides a belief that the other person will be true to you and will not deceive you at any point in life. Respect ensures the treatment everyone is going to receive in a relationship.

> *"Respect for ourselves guides our morals; respect for others guides our manners."*
> **- Laurence Sterne**

Trust plays a pivotal role in happy and successful relationships. It promotes positivity by allowing you to be more open and giving toward your counterpart/s. If you have trust, you know how the other person is and can ignore their shortcomings and faults. You become better at managing the conflicts because of that.

Trust brings people closer. It serves as a cornerstone for developing strong bonds and connections. It ensures a sense of safety and security among them. It also unites them and helps them work together to accomplish common goals.

On the other hand, respect is important while working for a healthy relationship. However, it is mostly overlooked, so many relationships break down.

Respect allows people to accept each other, communicate well, and build trust. It means admiring another person's qualities, wishes, opinions, and rights. It ensures feelings of trust, safety, and well-being in a relationship.

Trust and respect go hand in hand to build a strong and healthy relationship. Together, they help people accept others as and how they are. They develop confidence in one another and present their true selves without artificial layering, strengthening their bond.

II. Managing Conflicts and Misunderstandings

When people come close, their opinions differ, and the chance for conflicts becomes inevitable. Disagreements may take place, and that isn't necessarily a bad thing. Everyone has a right to choose and can hold different opinions. Being in a healthy relationship doesn't mean to curb your real personality and become what your counterpart is or wants you to be. Instead, being in a healthy relationship calls for a union of two (or more) partners/people who, even though they have different perspectives, are united, accepting everyone for who/how they are. It thrives on mutual respect and understanding for one another. Ultimately, it's the harmony between uniqueness and togetherness that defines a truly healthy and fulfilling relationship.

Conflict or misunderstanding in a relationship is normal. However, you must ensure that your arguments don't become personal attacks or efforts to lower others' self-esteem. What's important is that you communicate effectively, opting for a healthy way to resolve the issue. This will help you understand each other and strengthen your relationship.

Managing conflict is an art, and how you can learn that. Let me share some tips with you regarding that:

1. Create a welcoming environment so that everyone can communicate openly. You and your counterparts can talk freely about what is bothering you and how to work to improve your relationship. I suggest discussing your problems and the positives so one feels like they are going completely wrong. If you fear expressing your feelings, you must re-evaluate things and work on your relationship.
2. In a heated argument, ensure you are in control. Do not cross the line and start insulting the person you disagree with. Focus on the dispute and not bring personal jibes to put that person down. And this goes for both parties. Unless this thing is mutual, you can never find a solution to your problem.
3. Get to the root of the problem and find an adequate solution ASAP, rather than getting into prolonged discussion, research, or seeking additional help if required. Unnecessary arguments will only lead to distress, affecting the bond both parties share.
4. Learn "agreeing to disagree." If both parties cannot resolve an issue, it's better to drop it. Or if it's important, you can discuss it later when everything cools off and you all are in your sound mind. Don't exhaust yourself in the quest to find an immediate

solution. Time heals everything, and giving time may lead you to contemplate what you have been missing while arguing.
5. Compromising is a major part of resolving conflicts. It can be hard to achieve sometimes, but you must consider what is important. Find some middle ground and end your discussion. That's it!
6. If the issue seems irresolvable, throw it in the bin. Don't get in inessential fights that pose no positive outcome. Focus on the bond you are sharing and work on improving that. It is good for your mental and physical health as well.

Conflict resolution is not the responsibility of any one person. Rather, it is a shared task that should be done by all the parties involved. The tips that I have shared are for everyone. Whether you are romantic partners, living in a family, or having issues at your workplace, these will help you come out of that and arrive at a conclusion.

III. Nurturing Healthy Relationships

As you progress in life, you will realize that building a relationship is not enough; nurturing it to the point where it stays strong and healthy is the real task. I have seen people fail in relationships because they fail to take care of them properly.

Healthy relationships can enhance your life and make everyone feel good about themselves. However, they just don't happen themselves. Effort is required to take a relationship to that point.

Before we move forward on how to do that, let me list down the signs of healthy relationships:
- Respect
- Trust
- Open communication
- Equality
- Individual and shared interest
- Understanding
- Honesty

- Care
- Emotional support
- Common values

There are too few to list, but they are the most common ones. Match them with your life and see where you are lacking. Work on that, follow the tips I have mentioned, and do your research. I guarantee that the steps you take today to build strong and better relationships will help you a lot as you journey through the various phases of life, whether personal or professional.

Yet, it is essential to acknowledge that no relationship is flawless; achieving perfection requires dedication and patience, which comes over time. You are doing well as long as it doesn't put you under stress. How can I maintain a healthy relationship? This is the question I am going to answer now.

1. **Be clear in your words:** Communicating clearly helps nurture a healthy relationship. So, convey your point more clearly rather than choosing to be passive or aggressive in your interactions. The lack of clarity on what people want to say often hinders healthy relationships.
2. **Be respectful:** It is good to present your point, but it should be done respectfully. You must respect other people's values and points of view if you are aiming at creating a strong bond with him/her.
3. **Say sorry when wrong:** Human beings are prone to make mistakes. No one is perfect. So, say sorry and be apologetic when you are wrong. Don't act stubborn in that case. Saying sorry occasionally helps to heal the breakdowns in relationships that are inevitable to occur.
4. **Be affectionate:** Express your fondness or care for the person with whom you want to cultivate a strong bond. Prove it with your actions and behavior. Taking time to go out with that person, hugging them occasionally, and even sitting together and having long conversations will promote this feeling.
5. **Prioritize the relationship:** The person who holds a special position in your life comes first before everyone and everything.

Similarly, it sometimes becomes hard for those who work in professional settings to balance work and personal life. Set limits for your other interactions and establish a work-life balance if you want to achieve satisfaction in your life.
6. **Develop common interest:** Sharing similar hobbies or looking out for common ground of interest can strengthen your relationship. This way, you will enjoy being around the person/people and share moments that will ultimately improve your connection with them.
7. **Feel good about yourself:** When you start feeling good about yourself, you become more motivated and give your best to your relationships. Numerous studies have proven this psychological fact. Enjoy what you do most. If you feel happy and content from inside, you can transfer that same emotion into your relationships.
8. **Find common solutions:** Whenever you find yourselves in conflict, try to find a common solution by making joint efforts to resolve it. The more aptly you solve your disputes, the healthier your relationship will become.
9. **Plan for the future:** Sit with the person, make plans, and develop strategies for getting together.
10. **Give your time:** Time is the most valuable asset you can invest in strengthening your relationships. Spend quality time with the people you want to stay close to. Be it your family, spouse, children, friends, or colleagues, you are required to put in adequate effort.

Relationships are filled with challenges. They undergo ups and downs at various times, which is their beauty. It allows you to ponder and evaluate where you are falling short. It is also an opportunity to reconsider whether staying in that relationship affects you. If you feel it has failed to impact your life positively, then that is the correct time to come out of it. It's better to feel hurt for a while rather than be in long-lasting agony.

It's getting too serious, right? Let me cool it down for you. I believe that, at this stage, you may have a clear idea of how having relationships helps you progress positively. You also have learned the impact of negativity on human life and their relationships. Now, in the next chapter, we will discuss how to work on developing social skills that are useful in everyday interactions and communicating with others. Keep working on your progress like this, and I will see you there.

Key Takeaways

- We are social animals who cannot live alone.
- We need healthy relationships to flourish and grow.
- The way we behave, interact, and engage with other people shapes our relationships with them.
- Trust and respect are the two main aspects of a healthy relationship.
- These elements lead to people's acceptance of each other.
- Conflicts are certain in human relationships.
- With proper attention and necessary measures, disagreements can be resolved.
- Committing to a relationship is not child's play and requires ample effort.
- Healthy relationships enhance life and make people feel good about themselves.

Exercise

A short quiz to test your knowledge of how much you have understood.

a. What is the key characteristic distinguishing a platonic relationship from a romantic one?
    i. Physical intimacy
    ii. Emotional connection
    iii. Shared interests
    iv. Length of time known

b. Which of the following is NOT a type of relationship?
    i. Family
    ii. Friendship
    iii. Acquaintance
    iv. Competition

c. True or False: Trust is built solely on time spent together.

d. What is a fundamental component of respect in a relationship?
    i. Being agreeable at all times
    ii. Listening attentively
    iii. Ignoring differences
    iv. Always getting your way

e. What is a healthy way to address conflicts in a relationship?
    i. Ignoring the issue and hoping it will go away
    ii. Blaming the other person entirely
    iii. Communicating openly and honestly
    iv. Seeking revenge

f. Which of the following can contribute to misunderstandings in a relationship?
    i. Assuming the worst intentions
    ii. Lack of communication
    iii. Different cultural backgrounds
    iv. All of the above

g. What is a key aspect of nurturing a healthy relationship?
  i. Spending all your time together
  ii. Supporting each other's personal growth
  iii. Controlling each other's actions
  iv. Always prioritizing one person's needs over the other's

h. True or False: Healthy relationships require constant effort and attention from both parties.

Answer Key

a. Physical intimacy
b. Competition
c. False
d. Listening attentively
e. Communicating openly and honestly
f. All of the above
g. Supporting each other's personal growth
h. True

CHAPTER 5

Developing Social Skills

"We're losing social skills, the human interaction skills, how to read a person's mood, to read their body language, and be patient until the moment is right to make or press a point. Too much exclusive use of electronic information dehumanizes a very important part of community life and living together."

- Vincent Nichols

HAVE YOU EVER felt shy about talking to new people? Have you ever heard of the term "breaking the ice"? If you face difficulty interacting with people around you, your social skills need work.

In today's world, socializing and getting along with others are among the most important skills for young children to learn. These skills are used to communicate daily in various ways, whether verbal, nonverbal, written, or visual. Social skills are also called "interpersonal" or "soft skills."

As you grow older, you need to interact with others, be it with family, friends, colleagues, peers, or others; these skills help you do that. Moreover, these skills help you enhance your academic skills as well as help you grow physically as young and professionally as you become a man or a woman.

I. Networking and Making New Connections

In the previous chapter, we discussed the personal aspects of communication. Here, we will discuss social skills that will help you professionally. Soon, you will graduate and join a prestigious firm; if not, you might work part-time to support your expenses and studies; no matter where you are in the coming years, you will always need these skills to flourish and make something of yourself.

What is networking?

Simply put, networking is when you meet new people who are in your industry and share similar professions and interests. You interact with them and work toward building and maintaining relationships with them.

In the modern job market, networking and maintaining connections are stepping stones for sound professional growth. That said, it is not just about collecting a large number of contacts. Instead, it means building relationships and offering support, guidance, and avenues.

This is why networking is important

1. Networking can help you increase your social well-being and develop long-lasting friendships. You might think that networking is strictly professional, but let me tell you that numerous people have befriended each other in their workplaces and become lifelong friends. One of them is me. I met my best friend at one of the start-ups in 2017. Since then, we have been together, witnessing each other's successes and being part of one another's personal growth.
2. You can exchange and share ideas and try new things that assist you grow professionally. Listening to what other people do at their jobs to navigate challenges can inspire you to develop new techniques to be more efficient in your work.

Discussing your job with like-minded people offers a new perspective on things differently. With their guidance, you may learn tricks to solve what you have stuck at for a long time.
3. Networking can help you meet with people in senior positions and at the top levels of different companies. Accessing higher-ups is not possible in some organizations, and networking clears your way by connecting with them.

 Having people of different levels in your network can also pave paths for better career opportunities. With that, you can connect with people from different industries who can help you switch and explore different career options.
4. If you are shy or introverted, networking is best for gaining that lost confidence in life. It is the place to present your ideas and speak about things that matter to you. People here are cooperative, may understand your feelings, and will not judge you. Instead, they will help you face that and play a role in your development.
5. Networking expands your visibility. The more you engage with people, sharing your ideas and POVs (Points of View), the clearer you become. You polish your thought process and shrug off the minor confusions hindering your professional journey by reaching a definite conclusion.

Effective networking is a social skill that can speed up one's growth in the professional realm.

II. Social Etiquette in Various Settings

Developing social skills will not serve you well if you lack the necessary etiquette to be observed in various settings. In this part, I will discuss the manners to maintain during social interactions.

Social etiquette can be defined as the accepted codes of conduct displayed during human communications. You may learn most of these behaviors through experiences with other people ingrained in their cultures and considered "polite."

These manners help you build strong relationships with the people around you. It creates an environment where people feel comfortable while interacting with one another.

However, human society has reached a point where this etiquette has become a lost art. No one pays enough heed to that aspect; thus, we see many complex relationships around us. Proper social manners require following certain norms to live and coexist with others in harmony. People perceive and treat you according to your demeanor and how you move within a society.

Here are a few that could help you build trust and reliance, assisting you in building long-term relationships.

Chivalry: Be chivalrous. Open doors for ladies and offer them your seat. Treat older people with care and kindness.

Conscious: Be mindful of how you sit, walk, and talk when you are among people. Display your best behavior when you are surrounded by people.

Dress accordingly: Choose appropriate attire every time you go somewhere. Your dress code signifies your professionalism, respect, and social desirability.

Do small talk: Engage in small talk to signal you are friendly and not a threat. Choose topics that are unoffensive and will not get you in trouble.

Courteous: Practice courtesy by saying small phrases like "thank you" or "excuse me." If you are lost and need to ask directions, do it politely and show your appreciation.

Conformity: Conform with practices to adhere to the society. You will gain acceptance much quicker and easier because of that.

Punctual: Punctuality is a virtue that will help you in the long run. It is one of the virtues that is diminishing from our lives. By being punctual, you display that you care about other people's time and respect them. Try to apply that in your life.

Learn names: People feel delighted when you remember their name and even appreciate it when you get it right the first time. They feel that you care enough and are paying attention to them.

Limit phone usage: Limit using your people while eating or being in conversation with the people. Focus on conversing with your friends or family at the dinner table, and keep your phones away for a while.

III. Online Socializing: Do's and Don'ts

Socializing has now been limited to our physical connections, but it has become digital with the advent of social media in our lives. The internet has demolished the distances between different places and brought people belonging to different cultures and traditions closer to each other. Now, you don't need to go somewhere to learn about that place. Instead, you can send a Facebook friend request to someone who lives there and learn everything from them.

The use of social media is increasing rapidly, and the youth of our time comprises most of the world's population active on these platforms.

However, the digital world is not at all safe. It is more dangerous than the normal offline world. Digital communities are prone to online threats. People's increased accessibility makes them easy targets of malware, extortion scams, and identity thefts.

Here, you must think that if I am urging you, people, to leave, quit social media, and return to the stone age. It's not like that. Instead, I want you to use it wisely and learn what and what not should be practiced while spending your time on social media.

I have developed some strategies to protect my digital persona and well-being. It is as follows:

First of all, be careful of what you post on social media. Keep in mind what you post there can never be taken of. If your private information gets shared online, it is no longer private. You may post things that may seem harmless, but that's what the scammers are seeking. Online information can easily be copied, cached, or shared, so there is very little possibility that anything is ever completely removed.

When you receive any sort of link from your friend, don't click on it immediately. It may be malware sent by an imposter to steal your online identity.

Read the platforms' privacy policies and research the organization. Find out how your personal information will be used or monitored if you sign up with them. Read security tips, FAQs, and features information to learn about their websites' privacy and security controls. Clear your history and remove any caches or cookies to protect yourself for the future.

Avoid downloading third-party applications not available on official app stores offered by the operating system on your devices. These apps are not verified and may have malicious viruses and malware attached to them that infect your devices. This makes you more vulnerable to digital indecencies happening all around the world.

The digital world is getting dirty with every passing second. Therefore, it calls for people who come forward and work to make it a better place, especially for the young kids who plan on becoming part of it. If we start today, I hope we will very soon accomplish that goal and reshape what humanity is facing.

IV. Overcoming Shyness and Social Anxiety

Now, let us discuss how we can overcome our shyness and prevent ourselves from experiencing social anxiety. This will help us gain confidence in our lives and become proficient in our social interactions.

1. **Challenge your negative and anxious thoughts:** Analyze your thoughts and challenge them to make you feel that way. Ask yourself why you think that way. Was it your first reaction, or are you just assuming that? Change your thinking style.

Look for positivity around yourself. This will help you speed up what you are working to attain.

2. **Be mindful and meditate:** If you meditate and remain mindful of yourself and your surroundings, you may become more aware of your thoughts and feelings nonjudgmentally and positively.

Therapists suggest that meditation and mindfulness can not only help in reducing social anxiety but also play a vital role in lowering the effects of depression.

3. **Do what you what you like to do:** Engage in activities you like and feel comfortable with. Practice that in an environment where you usually get anxious. By doing so, you will be able to push yourself but remain in your mental comfort zone, diminishing social anxiety at the same time. Watch online movies and TV shows, go to your favorite coffee shop, or take a walk in a park; whatever you think reduces the negative feelings that come to your mind.
4. **Create an exposure hierarchy:** It is the best way to overcome your social anxiety. Figure out and rate how each social encounter makes you feel anxious. For example, 0 would mean no anxiety, and 10 would be extreme anxiety. Predict your behaviors in different situations to know how and what you feel whenever you face them.
5. **Don't focus on yourself:** Shift your focus from yourself and think about other things. Your constant mind chatter and questioning of how people will perceive you will do no good. Instead, it will make you more anxious and feel bad about yourself. Talk to other people and work on making genuine connections. Believe me, you just need to make an effort, and everything will follow automatically.
6. **Talk and face your fears:** Talk to people gradually. It will help you feel less anxious each time. Face your fears. It is impossible to overcome social anxiety if you don't expose yourself to the situations that make you anxious. You need to learn how to deal with it. Remember that we humans are social beings. Forcing yourself out of your comfort zone is necessary to increase your chance of a successful experience. Every situation you face and overcome will help boost your confidence.

At this point, I will wind up this chapter. I believe what I have tried to explain here will help you in the long run. These skills are not age-bound. Instead, they are going to serve you well as you journey through different phases of your life. In the next chapter, I am going to discuss another important thing with you: Time management and organization.

Share what you are learning with your friends and motivate them to practice these skills together.

Key Takeaways

- Socializing is one of the most important skills to be learned in these modern times.
- Social skills are also called "interpersonal" or "soft skills."
- These skills help not only in physical growth but also in mental well-being.
- Networking refers to developing connections with professionals within and outside the industry.
- Networking plays a vital role in career development.
- Learning social etiquette is as well as necessary as learning other skills.
- Respectfulness, politeness, kindness, etc., are some accepted social human manners.
- You need to follow the same code of conduct online as offline.
- You need to be extra cautious while using the internet.

Exercise

Fill in the blanks:

1. Social media platforms have bridged the gap between distant cultures and traditions, allowing people to connect regardless of physical distance. However, users must be cautious about the information they share, as once posted, it becomes _____.
2. To safeguard against online threats such as malware and identity theft, it is advisable to exercise caution when _____ links received from friends, as they may be sent by imposters with malicious intent.
3. Before signing up for any social media platform, it is essential to _____ the organization and carefully read their privacy policy to understand how personal information will be used or monitored.
4. To minimize the risk of malware and viruses, it is recommended to avoid downloading _____ applications from unofficial sources, as they can be harmful.
5. Parents and guardians play a crucial role in ensuring the online safety of children by _____ their online activities and guiding them to navigate the digital world responsibly.

Answers: 1. permanent 2. clicking on 3. research 4. third-party 5. monitoring

Make a Difference with Your Review
Essential Life Skills For Teens

"Teaching teens essential life skills is planting seeds of resilience that will bloom throughout their lives."   - Desmond Tutu

People who give without expectation live longer, happier lives and make more money.
So, if we've got a shot at that during our time together, darn it, I'm gonna try.
To make that happen, I have a question for you...
Would you help someone you've never met, even if you never got credit for it?

<u>Who is this person, you ask?</u> They are like you — or, at least, like you used to be — less experienced, wanting to make a difference, and needing help but not sure where to look.
<u>Our Mission?</u> To make Essential Life Skills accessible to everyone. That's the driving force behind everything I do. And the only way we can achieve that is by reaching out to... well, everyone!
This is where <u>You</u> come in. We often judge a book by its cover (and its reviews), right? So, on behalf of a struggling teen, you've never met:
Could you do us a solid by leaving a review for this book?

It'll take you less than a minute and won't cost a dime, but it could completely turn around a fellow teen's <u>LIFE</u>. Your <u>Review</u> might:

...Help a teen find ways to manage money.
...Assist a kid in navigating the job market.
...Support a student in managing their communication skills for success.
...Assist them in improving and building relationships.
...Make one more dream come true.

To get that <u>'feel good'</u> feeling and help this person for real, all you have to do is...and it takes less than <u>60 seconds...</u>

Leave a Review!

Simply scan the <u>QR code</u> below to leave your review:

https://www.amazon.com/review/review-your-purchases/?asin=BOOKASIN\

Feeling good about helping an <u>Anonymous Teen?</u> You are exactly my kind of person.
<u>Welcome</u> to the <u>Club. You're</u> one of <u>Us.</u>

I can't wait to share with you some <u>Fantastic Communication Strategies</u> and <u>Life-Changing Skills</u> in the Upcoming Chapters. Trust me; you're going to love them!

Thank you from the bottom of my heart. Now, back to our regularly scheduled programming.

Your biggest fan,

Emma Davis

CHAPTER 6

Time Management and Organization

"Our life is the sum total of all the decisions we make every day, and those decisions are determined by our priorities."

— **Myles Munroe**

SO, YOUNG ADULTS, the last chapter was completely about going out socially, knowing how to do things right, getting noticed, and possibly walking out of the poster. But now, let's switch gears to something equally important: time management and organization.

Here's the scoop: Have you ever been on your phone for what felt like five minutes, but when you looked up, you realized it was five hours? Of course, we have all been in this situation at some point. It's just as if time is a mischievous creature that always likes to play games with you. However, do not panic, as this paragraph will take you deep into the jungle of time management.

Perhaps you will ask yourself, "What is the benefit of planning my day?" "I'm way too immersed in being a social butterfly!" Ok, hold your boots because mastering this thing will not just lead you to solely be a productivity guru. This is all about being able to spend more time pursuing things that make you happy without the feeling that you are sinking under the weight of never-ending deadlines and tasks.

Then, hold on and get ready to receive the secrets of killing the schedule, turning procrastination into a boss, and creating a balance between work and play. Well, then give it a try, and you'll find yourself making the best out of time, as you've never done before. Let's dive in!

I. Prioritizing and Planning Your Day

Imagine this: Here you are, your to-do list goes up to the mountain, and each task is begging for your attention patiently like a pet. And without prioritization, it would be absolute chaos, with you running around like a headless chicken trying to do everything at once. However, it would just end up in a total disaster. Sound familiar?

However, don't be afraid anymore, as prioritizing will come to the rescue! It feels like getting an enchanted wizard hat for your list of tasks, telling where you should devote your attention and efforts first of all.

Imagine it as your magic trick for handling the stress of daily life. By arranging those tasks hierarchically, you're not just subduing your workload but also creating more space to indulge in your favorite series or tackle the world (whatever you fancy).

Here's how you do it.

Step 1: Offload It Like It's On Fire: The first and foremost thing is to get your favorite notebook or use the usual smartphone application to dump all these tasks your mind is full of. All the daily and weekly stuff, even the things you plan to tackle next month – get it all out there. It is like a brain dump that has no mess.

Step 2: Choose Your Battles Carefully: Now, not every task is born equal. Some are like unruly small gremlins who demand your immediate attention, while others are such distant cousins that you forget to call. So, ask yourself: Who's gonna weep for this project if it is not completed by tomorrow? What benefit do you get when completing the work? The most important question here is, what will happen if you don't? We've got to sort the wheat from the chaff, you all.

Step 3: Establish Your Priorities First: Okay, so your tasks are all lined up in order like obedient troops. Now what? It is the time to use your perfect strategy. You may eat frogs, sort through the Eisenhower Matrix, or simply ABCDE your way to success. At the end of the day, find a technique that resonates with you and consistently apply it. Believe me, it's just like having a cheat code for your task list.

a. **The Eisenhower Matrix:** Have you ever gotten wrapped up in overwhelming tasks, just being clueless about which one you want to deal with first? Welcome to the "Eisenhower Matrix," an innovator in the arena of priorities. Imagine a small grid that goes "Important" on one side and "Not Important" on the other, finishing with "Urgent" and "Not Urgent" on the top and bottom. Put your activities into these four groups, and there you have it – instant clarity! From crucial to less time-critical, this matrix shows you what to do, what to postpone, what to abbreviate, and what to throw away forever.

b. **The ABCDE Method:** Say, let's make an alphabet game for your to-do list. What do you say? For the ABCDE method, A would be the shining musical star, and E is the last stand-up comedian you would avoid by all means. Whether by yourself or with a group, this technique brings out the best in you by giving a definite structure to your road to victory. Despite not being its specialty, it is a master in getting the essentials done and leaving out the 'maybe-later' issues.

c. **Eat the Frog:** Have you ever heard about the sentence "eating the frog"? This sentence has nothing to do with going down to the pond to eat frog legs. It's about swallowing that huge, scary pill to get it over and done with once and for all right away. Why? This is because, when you have swallowed that frog, the remaining chores for the rest of the day never feel like mountains to climb. No more dodging the serious business – just productivity in its natural state.

d. **The MIT Method:** Target a few items that you are excited about and dedicated to from the to-do list. The rest of the to-do list will wait until you pamper yourself first. It's like cutting through the fog for your creativity to take off, maintaining your schedule, and taming your stress simultaneously.

Step 4: Schedule Like a Boss: Listen, your calendar is not just for doctors' appointments and lunch with your friends. It is also the way to conquer the obstacles of task-taming. Thus, look at what is scheduled for the next day and see if it covers your priorities. Otherwise, sorting needs to be done. Oh, and don't forget to make some space for the unexpected – task warriors need breaks, too.

Step 5: Confront Your Fears: Alright, it's time for some real talk: Those enormous, petrifying tasks are not going to take care of themselves. Therefore, instead of burying your head in the sand (or your Instagram feed), just grab that frog by its' legs and take a big giant bite. Believe me, when you've taken the beast down, everything else will seem like a piece of cake. Besides, there is an opportunity to share your accomplishments.

II. Overcoming Procrastination and Distractions

You know, the besetting voice in your mind that says, "I'll do it later," which then becomes never.

Simply put, procrastination means to put off to a later point in time what should be done immediately or promptly. It's like hitting the snooze button in life – postponing or avoiding all those tasks that should have been tackled long ago, whether it's as boring as dwelling on trivialities or as terrifying as confronting a dragon.

Let's face it: We've all had that experience at least once in our lives. From skipping school assignments because they are like the plague to just letting our laundry pile up until it rivals the height of Mount Everest, procrastination is the ultimate time thief.

In short, these postponed tasks do not go away on their own but rather remain hidden. They like to remind us that we procrastinate by whispering our sins into our ears.

Alright, get your swords and shields ready. We are about to slay the procrastination monster together for good!

First, let's take a look at the factors that make us professional procrastinators.

1. **The Boredom Blues:** Have you ever encountered such a mundane activity that you'd rather watch a paint dry? Yeah, we've all passed through it. Often, the tasks that you find most exciting are the ones you would rather do over anything else.
2. **The Irrelevance Riddle:** Picture this: you find yourself in a situation when you are given a job, but instead of thinking, "Ok, here I go!" you ask, "Why bother?" When something is not as cool as breathing the same air with dinosaurs, it is challenging to find the necessary excitement even to try to complete it.
3. **The Confidence Crisis:** Self-doubt is the ultimate party spoiler. When we don't feel the superheroes, we're supposed to be, snoozing the tasks is too easy. Ultimately, many of us would rather point fingers at ourselves than face the uncertainty of not meeting the mark.
4. **The Goalless Gambit:** Have you ever felt that you have been sailing around without any definite idea of where you are heading? When a deadline or a goal is not a constant source of motivation, it is simple to engage in procrastination practices and later reason, "I will do it tomorrow."

Here are three tools to beat procrastination:

1. Self-Determination Theory: Boost your motivation by understanding what drives and hinders you.
2. Personal Mission Statements: Add purpose to your task for increased enthusiasm.
3. Cognitive Restructuring: Reframe negative thoughts to overcome procrastination.

And that's it – everything that makes us kings of procrastination. However, do not be afraid because, with this knowledge in hand, we are one step closer to turning procrastination into a thing of the past and becoming productive. Holding on to these strategies, we can withstand procrastination and regain productivity.

1. **Time Management Magic:** Walk into the ring armed with time management tactics with a clear aim. You can apply one of these tricks, Eisenhower Box or timeboxing, and make your checklist from intimidating to manageable without any effort.
2. **Cling to the 2-Minute Rule:** Have you ever heard of the 2-minute rule? It's like a magic wand to cast away procrastination. If a task takes less than two minutes, do not postpone it. Conquer it right away and see how your list of tasks becomes more and more manageable.
3. **Practice your self-discipline:** It is high time that we use self-control and make procrastination surrender its throne. However, it is not about pushing yourself to do things you hate. Instead, develop mindful resolutions and observe how your productivity will rise.
4. **Distraction Defense:** Name the distractions that can defeat you and give them the impossible mission of slipping into your workspace. It can be managing distractions by turning off notifications or creating a Zen-like environment, the key to remaining focused.
5. **Break It Down:** Break down your tasks into smaller, digestible parts, and the feeling of being overwhelmed will disappear. Take one small step at a time, and then you will be unstoppable and conquer the mountains like a pro.

From now on, you are equipped with everything you need to fight procrastination and regain your productivity rule.

III. Effective Study and Work Habits

Do you feel ready to boost your productivity capacity? How about exploring the universe of learning and working habits to help you become a goal-crushing master?

1. **Build Your Ideal Location to Study:** Selecting the right study place makes or breaks your productivity and learning. Choose a place with good lighting and ample space where your mind can

be stimulated and your surroundings do not distract you. Forget about dim corners and narrow rooms – it's time for brightness and the best focus of your study space.
2. **Unleash Your Productivity:** Add glamour to your study regimen by infusing creativity into your working space. From the motivational posters to the brightly colored sticky notes and the convenient flashcards, let these things around you fuel the fire of your desire to learn.
3. **Immerse Yourself in the Topics of Your Interest:** For the start of your study sessions, ditch your textbooks and classes and tune your mind to your most enjoyed learning topics. Whether you are a math genius or a grammar expert, dig deep to find out what gets you inspired in academic terms.
4. **Compose a Study Plan for 21 Days:** Plan your learning reading schedule with a 21-day duration in which each day will help you track your progress and stay on the right track. Set up your goal and divide your tasks into interactive pieces. Stay on track and work to attain your academic prowess on a daily basis.
5. **Nurture Curiosity and Ask Everything:** Be driven by curiosity in your study sessions by asking questions, reacting to others' questions, and engaging in discussions. Immerse yourself into areas of interest, challenge the existing opinions, and enjoy the excitement of critical reasoning. You will change idle moments into learning and discovery chances by cultivating your curiosity.
6. **Indulge Yourself with Deserved Rewards:** Leverage positive reinforcement by rewarding yourself for a job properly done. Develop achievable study goals and make sure that every break is filled with social media, walking leisurely, and eating yummy treats.
7. **Test Yourself:** Practice tests before and after studying can lead to improved memory and the identification of knowledge gaps. The strobe effect is when you recall information, and it resets your "forgetting clock" and strengthens your learning.

Now that you have the winning strategies, your study times will be transformed into effective powerhouses where learning flourishes and success performs exceptionally.

IV. Balancing School, Work, and Personal Life

While coping with challenges like work, school, and personal life, we need to be aware of work-life balance. This balance is represented by the continuous back-and-forth collision between our work duties and commitments to home and family.

> **An unhealthy work-life balance occurs when work overwhelms personal life, leading to:**
> - Constant overwork
> - Neglected Personal Life
> - Burnout
> - Lack of Self-care
> - Strained Relationships

According to Barlett et al. (2021), striking a perceived sense of balance between work and life represents a challenge for many in academic and research sectors worldwide.

Let's discuss the ways of balancing these different aspects of our lives and giving priority to our well-being during a busy life.

1. **Strategize with a Plan:** Plan out your days first to stay on the right track and focused. Having free time might be overwhelming, so writing down your class and work hours, study time, and social activities in the weekly calendar is a good idea. When feeling overloaded, pick out small, manageable tasks, like spending a snatch of time on studies during commutes or planning meals for busy weeks ahead of time.

2. **Stay on Track:** Test out different schedules and choose the one that suits you best. Eliminate procrastination by reserving time exclusively for assignments and starting to work immediately.
3. **Lean on Support:** A full-time job with school can be difficult, but a supportive network can help relieve the tension. Tell your loved ones your schedule and get their support. Give back by responding through good communication and compromise, too.
4. **Focus on Goals:** If you are feeling exhausted, visualize your aims. It depends on whether student debt is offset or a family is supported while pursuing a degree. The vital thing to remaining concentrated on the big picture is to get motivated.
5. **Embrace Multitasking:** Organize your work well to maximize time utilization and produce multipurpose output. Build activities that involve shopping and working out with family members to ensure quality time and productivity go hand in hand. Make the most of your commute time by learning new things or performing tasks that engage your whole family.
6. **Prioritize Essential Activities:** Select and reduce trivial tasks that demand a lot of time. Avoid activities such as checking your private emails or surfing the Internet, as they can interfere with your productivity. Narrow down on activities that are in line with your goal.
7. **Nurture Personal Well-being:** You can set aside some time for hobbies and self-care activities to relieve stress from your life. Spend time doing stuff you like, reading a book, or exercising to freshen up your mind and body. Invest in healthy habits such as nutritious eating and adequate sleep to bolster overall well-being.

With these tips, you can successfully manage the school, work, and personal spheres while caring about your overall well-being.

Key Takeaways

- Create a list of priorities based on what tasks must be completed first. Employ calendars and timetables.
- Recognize procrastination triggers and develop strategies to overcome them. Divide tasks into smaller, manageable pieces that make you feel less overwhelmed.
- Distractions should be minimized by providing a good study or work environment.
- Develop a productive routine so as not to lose focus and stay structured.
- Make a timetable and work on accomplishing tasks to avoid procrastination. Remove distractions to improve attention and work efficiency.
- Think ahead by planning and managing your schedule without overloading.
- Create a support network by sharing your schedule and explaining your needs with friends and family.
- Concentrate on your goals so you never lose sight of your motivation. Do multiple tasks intelligently to maximize time and efficiency.
- Set boundaries, practice self-care, and communicate effectively to maintain a healthy balance.

Exercise

Checklist

Instructions: For every statement, put a tick in the appropriate column describing whether the statement best matches or is not characteristic of you. The scale runs from (1) 'Not like me at all' to (5) 'Very similar to me.' Point (3) is neutral - neither typical nor unlike you. Then, based on your responses, evaluate whether you are a procrastinator!

STATEMENTS	Not like me at all	Not like me	Neither like me nor unlike me	Like me	Very like me
I often find myself performing tasks I intended to do days before.					
When planning a meeting, I make the necessary arrangements well in advance.					
I generally return emails and phone calls promptly.					
I find that jobs often don't get done for days, even when they require nothing except sitting down and doing them.					
Once I have the information I need, I usually make decisions as soon as possible.					

When I have something difficult to do, I tell myself it's better to wait until I feel more inspired.						
I usually have to rush to complete tasks on time.						
I usually start a task shortly after it's assigned to me.						
When deadlines are approaching, I often waste time by doing other things.						
I often have a task finished sooner than necessary.						
When preparing for a meeting, I am seldom caught having to do something at the last minute.						
I often delay starting tasks that I have to do.						
When faced with a huge task, I figure out what the first step is so that I can get going.						
I frequently say, "I'll do it tomorrow."						

CHAPTER 7

Problem-Solving And Critical Thinking

"The only way to solve a problem is to confront it head-on."

- Zig Ziglar

CHAPTER 7 COVERED overcoming procrastination while efficiently balancing our lives, much like a circus performer spinning plates. But what if those plates came crashing down, leaving us knee-deep in problems? Cheer up. Chapter 8 gives us the splendid weapon of problem-solving and the shield of critical thoughts. Therefore, tighten your seat belts, sharpen your pens, and be ready to conquer problems you are destined to overcome as a hero!

I. Identifying And Analyzing Problems

In the problem-solving journey, the first step is often the most crucial: referring to the community's problem and finding a solution to this problem. It feels like going on a treasure hunt when the treasure is a solution, but the map is hidden within the confounding facets of the problem itself. Let us look into the art of problem identification and analysis, where every challenge is a puzzle to be solved. Let's look at the following step-by-step approach to overcoming problems effectively.

1. **Identify the Problem:** All right, let's begin by spotlighting the offender. Let us dive into the detective's world and discover the problem's real cause. Grab your magnifying glass and ask yourselves: What's the deal here? Remember that the first thing you must do to eliminate the problem is recognize it.
2. **Define the Goals:** Now that we have found your problem, it's time to prepare your goals. What is your objective? Set your goals passionately, and let's set a course and sail to them as true champions.
3. **Explore Potential Solutions:** Let the creativity flow like a waterfall! It's brainstorm time, where no idea is too wild, and no solution is off the table. Hey, try to see beyond the box. Look inside the box. Why not explore that box, too? You will have various options to approach and beat your problems in your face.
4. **Choose and Implement a Solution:** Shake off your cape and prepare for action because you are sliding into the implementation mode with your head held high. Having a plan and being determined to carry out an operation.
5. **Evaluate the Outcome:** Lights, camera, evaluation! First of all, take a step back and ponder your journey. Did it work out? What went wrong, or what did you learn throughout? Let's take the chance to boost your problem-solving skills and come out of it even stronger than you were before!

Here you go! You are all solution-finders who can handle any obstacle that gets in your way. Using teamwork, creativity, and just a hint of resilience, no problem is unbeatable. Nothing can stop us from going out of there and winning over those problems.

II. Creative And Logical Solution Strategies

Welcome to the ultimate problem-solving resource—this guide. Just as a master craftsman without the right tools cannot build a masterpiece, problem-solvers without different approaches cannot penetrate the most difficult challenges. Here, we'll examine some distinctive problem-solving approaches that share a common goal but employ different techniques. From the rational classic method to creative brainstorming, be ready to broaden your problem-solving horizons to the level of an expert in this field. Therefore, let's take a plunge.

1. **The Rational Approach:** Let's start with the classics, then! The rational approach is like following a recipe—step by step until you've concocted the perfect solution. These steps will help you to pinpoint the problem, generate solutions, and pick the best.
2. **The Creative Approach:** It's the time to let your brightest creativity out of the closet! The creative solving approach focuses instead on crazy ideas and unusual thinking. Let me update you with some creative problem-solving methods:

> **Three real-life examples of Creative problem-solving:**
>
> **Netflix:** Initially struggling to attract viewers, Netflix developed a recommendation algorithm based on user preferences, revolutionizing personalized content delivery.
> **NASA:** Facing a crisis during the Apollo 13 mission, NASA engineers improvised a solution using available materials to fit a square CO_2 filter into a round hole, ensuring the safe return of astronauts to Earth.
> **IKEA:** To address challenges entering the Japanese market, IKEA innovated by creating furniture tailored for smaller places, successfully appealing to Japanese preferences.

   a. **Brainstorming:** Gather a group of people who can contribute knowledge from varied areas and generate multiple ideas that result from the human creative potential.
   b. **Reverse Thinking:** Look at the problem from a different angle by reversing the gaping hole or examining a perspective that is not commonly acknowledged. This can result in surprising, unconventional solutions.

    c. **SCAMPER Technique:** Sometimes, to spark creativity and inventiveness, you need to ** Change, Join, Adapt, Modify, Divert, Cut out, and Change standpoint elements.
    d. **Storyboarding:** Develop a path that leads to the issue approached. To do this, get people to fully understand the issue and devise creative solutions.
    e. **Role Play:** Take a step into the different personalities or perspectives associated with the problem to see things from another angle and generate the best innovative ideas.
3. **The Historical Approach:** Why create a new wheel when you can learn from past experiences? The historical approach goes back to the archives to develop solutions from the past to today's problems. It is like a voyage to the past to get the answers you seek.
4. **The Simplex Approach:** When the challenge is unfathomable, the simplex process stands tall to the occasion! Employing it, you will successfully navigate the unknown, starting with problem-finding and implementing the plan.
5. **The Collaborative Approach:** Have you ever heard the phrase "two heads are better than one"? With everybody collaborating, the team of a problem generator, problem finder, and problem solver is formulated. They will brainstorm, bounce, and weave ideas until a solution is found. Prove that there's nothing like working together in a team!
6. **The Logical Approach:** So, the Logical Approach should not be missed out on at all. With the spirit of Sherlock Holmes, who solves a case, I will help you apply logic and reason to the problem and discover the hidden truth. Are you ready to sit on top of your logic skills and follow clues? But wait, let's address some logical problem-solving methods first:
    a. **Root Cause Analysis:** Identify the problem's root causes by thoroughly searching for its origins and corresponding factors.
    b. **Ask WHY:** Continuously ask "why" to delve deeper into the root cause of the problem and uncover underlying issues.

    c. **Pareto Principle (80/20 Rule):** Focus actions on the essential few factors that have the most significant effect on the problem to achieve the most out of available resources.

    d. **SWOT Analysis:** Conducting a SWOT analysis of the issue within the case will identify the key strengths, weaknesses, opportunities, and threats. These findings will allow me to develop a more comprehensive understanding of the problem and formulate strategic solutions.

    e. **Systematic Problem-Solving Frameworks:** Take structured problem-solving methods relative to the scientific method, DMAIC (Define, Measure, Analyze, Improve, Control), and TRIZ (Theory of Inventive Problem Solving) to seek solutions to complicated matters.

7. **The Failure Mode and Effects Analysis (FEMA):** Why give trouble a chance to happen? FEMA intervenes to nip them in the bud by identifying and assessing the vulnerabilities ahead of time. This is like having a problem solver insurance that keeps you one step ahead of trouble.

8. **The Means-End Approach:** Occasionally, you have to begin with the finished product in mind. Through means-end analysis, we learn to concentrate on the target and move forward, overcoming barriers to reach our location. It's a road map for problem-solving!

9. **The Organic Approach:** Who says problems have to be played according to rules? The organic approach accepts complexity and lets issues develop on their own. It is an alternative way to overcome challenges—the journey is just as important as the destination.

10. **The Hybrid Approach:** Why settle for one when you can enjoy them all? A hybrid approach seizes the virtues of both methods, providing us with a toolbox for expanding problem-solving skills. A bit of imagination and a pinch of logic will get you to the perfect resolution anytime!

Here is your answer—problem-solving strategies and their methods to solve the problems coming your way. With some imagination, lots of collaboration, and tons of perseverance, there is no puzzle that you cannot solve!

IV. Decision-Making in Complex Situations

Often, we struggle to make decisions, and this is true, especially when confronted with complex and multi-disciplined situations. In these circumstances, our options can extend far, making it essential to implement decision-making thoughtfully and strategically. Whether dealing with intricate managerial problems or combating personal issues, the knowledge of decision-making in complex situations is crucial for making the right choices and achieving the best possible outcomes. This chapter will help you to understand and implement decision-making approaches that enable you to face complex environments with confidence and sharpness of mind.

Decision-making, in general, is a mental activity that involves selecting an appropriate solution from multiple options. It encompasses examining data, weighing possibilities, assessing consequences, and deciding among the alternatives according to goals, values, and interests.

Uncertainty is the main factor that makes informed decision-making difficult. It generates a vast amount of uncertainty, which often does not allow us to make sound decisions and increases the stress levels of decision-makers. Here's how uncertainty influences decision-making:

- **Increased Risk Aversion:** In the face of uncertainty, decision-makers prefer safer options and are reluctant to choose innovative alternatives with higher risks.
- **Difficulty in weighing the pros and cons:** Uncertainty makes comparing the options more difficult, as projecting the results becomes problematic without definite information.
- **Incomplete Information:** Lacking or short of data, decision-makers rely on assumptions, which leads to shortcomings in the information used.

- **Increased Complexity:** Complexity becomes the hallmark of uncertainty, as it encompasses various aspects, alternative outcomes, and possible consequences.
- **Inability to Decide:** Uncertainty can arise, and indecisiveness can be induced among decision-makers as they cannot pinpoint the best possible choice or fear making the wrong choice. Handling uncertainty, which is sometimes challenging in decision-making, calls for resilience and adaptability of decision-makers. One should take proactive steps in risk mitigation, complexity management, and taking up ambiguity in arriving at informed decisions. Let me update you with some strategies for decision-making under deep certainty:
- **Define Your Goals:** This can be done by identifying goals and maintaining their coherence with the organization's strategic objectives. When aiming for desired outcomes, you may eliminate some options you don't need and choose others that match your aspiration for success.
- **Gather Information:** Compile all possible internal and external data to make your decision-making well-founded. Total research and examination of all factors help decision-makers make fully informed choices.
- **Identify and Assess Alternatives:** Make a complete list of possible answers, including proposing, studying alternative approaches, and brainstorming to aid thinking. Evaluate the strengths and weaknesses of each alternative that will be determined, considering the cost, the level of risk, the capability of each option, and the level of impact it may have.
- **Flexibility and Agility:** Manage flexibility and agility in the situation and instantly change decision-making in response to the dynamics and changes in circumstances.
- **Collaboration:** Unite with your shifts, planning to work with your colleagues, experts, and others interested in the same thing to explore opportunities through diverse perceptions and opinions.
- **Embrace Uncertainty:** Integrate unpredictability as an inherent element in decision-making, cultivating tranquility with the

unknown and enlarging resolve to make decisions that took place in the past.
- **Make a Decision:** Go through the alternatives to help you reach your goals and achieve the highest degree of success. With a clear and definite choice, an effective decision can be made with the least costly and time-consuming revisions.
- **Take Action:** Explain and inform every one of the outcomes you've reached regarding its implementation and progress. Analyze results and provide feedback on the spot. If something needs to be changed, be ready to make those changes based on past experiences.

These tips will enable you to confidently face difficult decision making processes and ultimately achieve profound success.

BENEFITS OF INFORMED DECISION-MAKING

- Improved Efficiency
- Better Decision Quality
- Greater Clarity
- Proactive Problem-Solving

By following these strategies, you can confidently navigate complex decision-making processes, maximize the effectiveness of your choices, and contribute to organizational success.

V. Learning from Mistakes and Failures

"Learn from every mistake because every experience, encounter, and particularly your mistakes are there to teach you and force you into being more of who you are."

- Oprah Winfrey

Mistakes are the little imperfections and missteps that make us unique and interesting. They're the turns in the road we least expect in our lives, professionally and personally. Sometimes, we laugh at their absurdity. Sometimes, we sigh and ask ourselves why we got into that mess.

Let's take a quirky world tour through the world of mishaps and failures, where accidents and mistakes are building blocks for success and wisdom. After all, the best success comes from the ashes of failures in the beautiful chaos we call life. Let us take a step back: Do errors give us advantages? So yes, but this is only the case if you follow these steps after an error:

1. **Acknowledge Errors:** Start by having the courage to admit your errors and wrongdoings instead of completely covering them up. If an apology is required, please remember to be honest and accountable. Integrity and responsibility are the hallmarks of a courageous person who people willingly follow.
2. **Reframe and Analyze:** Turn your mind around to look for the essence of the whole world. Think about what was wrong, why, and how things could be changed to become more resilient.
3. **Engage in Self-Reflection:** Digging deeper and asking challenging questions to identify the events before the error was made will help recognize the problem. Accepting your mistakes is the first step to changing them.
4. **Implement Lessons Learned:** Translate insights to how best to target your audience by adjusting accordingly for what you have learned. Consistency is essential for stable progress, so you should exercise regularly to consolidate your improvements and increase your skill level.
5. **Assess Progress:** Be diligent in tracking your path toward achievements, either alone through self-evaluation or with the help of an accountability partner. Their objective viewpoint may feed the invaluable recommendation.
6. **Embrace Vulnerability:** Set aside the fear of making mistakes because, as experience has taught us, mistakes are an inevitable part of the learning process. Using self-esteem to open up is

one effective way to improve oneself both professionally and personally.
7. **Empower Change and Acceptance:** Realize that it is okay to make mistakes in a constantly evolving world. Learn to accept the way things are, ask for help, and remember that you are not alone in facing challenges.

So, you see, by viewing mistakes as a space for growth and upbringing, you will be able to nudge resilience, adaptation, and strength into your response to adversity. Without further ado, let me tell you how your mistakes can turn you into a resilient person!

- **Opportunities for Growth:** The gap between making and correcting a mistake is an opportunity to cultivate more knowledge with no purpose but to continue improving. Embracing errors develops a growth mindset, where failures are seen as stepping stones to success instead of roadblocks.
- **Enhanced Problem-Solving Skills:** Facing failures directly spurs you to think analytically and creatively about finding the cause and the solution. This transforms you into a resilient person as the challenges are effectively solved through the skills you have developed.
- **Increased Self-Awareness:** Making mistakes leads to higher self-understanding, which helps you recognize your strengths and weaknesses and provides opportunities to learn. This sense of self provides room for resilience in problem-solving, developing new skills, and dealing with obstacles instead of running away from them.
- **Strengthened Coping Mechanisms:** Making a mistake isn't a big deal, but it can help you train and develop healthier ways to deal with stress and adversity. Resilient people tend to be committed to acquiring the courage to face challenges with zeal.
- **Heightened Emotional Intelligence:** Making mistakes is a natural part of the learning process. It entails emotional control of oneself and those around one and staying objective and nonjudgmental. Consequently, making

mistakes and learning emotionally enhances emotional resilience by increasing a person's adaptability and flexibility in the face of hardships.

To sum up, errors are neither failures nor demerits but sources of learning and adaptability. Once you have admitted to your mistakes, reframed them as lessons, and accepted them, you will be able to build resilience, adaptability, and strength, hence being able to withstand difficult times with courage and resilience.

Now that you have learned problem-solving and critical thinking skills, it is your turn to delve into your health and well-being complexities. So go on, then. Make a difference in your community today. Turn to the next page!

Why is Resilience Important?

- Boosts Self Satisfaction
- Enhances Self-Esteem
- Frames Challenges as learning opportunities.
- Improves Communication
- Fuels Innovation

Key Takeaways

- Identify and analyze problems by defining the goals, exploring potential solutions, selecting and executing a solution, and evaluating an outcome.
- There are many approaches to problem-solving, such as the rational, logical, and creative approaches.
- Creative problem-solving methods include brainstorming, the SCAMPER technique, reverse thinking, storyboarding, and role play.

- Strategies for informed decision-making include defining your goals, gathering information, identifying and evaluating options, flexibility, collaboration, and much more
- To turn your mistakes into benefits, you must acknowledge your errors, reframe and analyze them, engage in self-reflection, and much more.
- Learning from mistakes can make you resilient because it provides growth opportunities, enhanced problem-solving skills, increased self-awareness, and more.

Exercise: "Mistakes as Masterpieces"

Objective: Reframe how you view mistakes and failures as opportunities for growth and learning.

Instructions:

- Provide yourself and your friends with a piece of paper and art supplies (markers, crayons, colored pencils, etc.).
- Think of a mistake or failure you have experienced recently, whether personally or professionally.
- Visualize this mistake as a blank canvas and use the art supplies to represent it creatively. You can draw, paint, or use artistic methods to depict your mistake.
- Reflect on the following questions as you all create your artwork:
  - What did I learn from this mistake or failure?
  - How has it helped me grow or develop as a person?
  - What positive outcomes have emerged as a result?
- Once you have completed your artwork, share your creations with the group. Explain the story behind your artwork and the lessons you have gained from your mistakes.
- Conclude the activity by encouraging participants to display their "Mistakes as Masterpieces" artwork somewhere visible as a reminder of the positive outcomes that can arise from adversity.

CHAPTER 8

Personal Health and Wellness

FOR THE MOMENT, the word of the day is – yourself. With greater health and wellness, you will find yourself more alive. It's about the lessons of your wellness since keeping a high-functioning machine and taking good care of your body and mind are equally important. In this chapter, I will share the foods and exercises that are good for you. We will further talk about what it takes to be healthy and fit. Hence, take up these essentials to keep yourself feeling and looking great!

I. Basics of Nutrition and Exercise

Diet and exercise are two crucial pillars in the journey toward a healthier lifestyle. These factors are usually bound together; they are versatile and are behind the maintenance of not only physical but also mental health. You can imagine this as a balanced scale, with one side representing nutrition and the other being exercise.

Why do we need this balance? Well, let's get into it. At the same time, most of us know that eating a decent, healthy diet coupled with regular exercise is not just about losing or gaining weight but also about being healthy. It is about growing your body and mind, encouraging better sleep, and lightening your mood.

Indeed, when you feed your body the appropriate nutrients and participate in physical activities, you are not just maintaining your weight. You are also enhancing brain function and overall health.

Hence, it's about what you consume and how you move your body. By incorporating a harmonious diet plan and grueling but health-conscious exercise regime, you will be working toward developing your physical health and cultivating your overall well-being. So, now the time has come to learn some secrets of balanced nutrition and exercise to unlock the door to being healthy and happy.

Eat Healthy

For every balanced diet, diversifying your diet should be a prerequisite for a healthy diet. Eating fruits, vegetables, whole grains, lean animal protein, and healthy fats gives the body the necessary nutrients that make it healthy and stronger.

Have a healthy breakfast!

- Choose whole-grain cereals and add protein like milk or nuts.
- Use whole-grain flour for pancakes or waffles, and add cottage cheese.
- Opt for whole-grain toast with protein like eggs or peanut butter.

Keep a Food Diary

A food diary is more than a simple record-keeping tool. It can be a game-changer for improving your eating habits. You realize this once you put a pen on paper and note down what you eat and drink. Consequently, you arrive at a profound knowledge of nutrition that you can employ to achieve the intended goal.

Hydrate for Health

Water intake is the very essence of doing good for the human body. The process of drinking enough water during your day-to-day routine will help you bypass the negative effects that come from dehydration.

Opt for Whole Foods

Processed foods can be convenient and time-saving, but they are frequently empty of necessary nutrients and can lead to health problems. However, you must stick with whole and unprocessed foods such as fruits, vegetables, and whole grains to fuel your body and promote good health.

Increase Eating Fruits and Vegetables

They contain exceptional distributions of vitamins, minerals, and fibers. Taking on different colorful fruits and vegetables to your diet aids in fighting off illnesses, improving digestion, and reducing the risk of chronic diseases.

Benefits of Exercise

- Keeps your mind sharp
- Helps you feel better
- Fights weight gain
- Lowers your risk of disease

Start Small with Exercise

One doesn't have to be overwhelmed by starting an exercise routine. Begin with an attainable goal, such as taking short walks or doing short workouts a few times a week.

EFFECTS OF POOR NUTRITION AND PHYSICAL INACTIVITY:

- Constipation
- Anemia
- Type 2 Diabetes
- Heart Disease
- Stroke
- Declining Mental Health
- Vision Problems

Find Your Exercise Partner

Working out jointly with a friend or family makes exercises more fun, and the person can be a source of encouragement. When it comes to keeping yourself on track and consistently working out, look for someone similar to you in terms of health and/or fitness.

Mix Up Your Workouts

Add variety to your workout routine to keep yourself stimulated and enhance results. Try various sports like strength training, cardio, and yoga to help test your body and keep you entertained.

Integrate Exercise into Daily Life

Exercise is an essential part of your daily routine, so make it a part of your schedule. In whatever way possible, i.e., a morning walk, a lunchtime yoga exercise, or an evening gym session, you must find an appropriate time that best suits you and be faithful to it.

Monitor Your Fitness Journey

Monitor your progress to keep track of your fitness routine. You can use a workout journal or a fitness app to do this. Tracking your progress in a certain category can help you stay motivated and focus on your goals.

Never Give Up

Above all, always maintain a positive mindset to maintain the best health. Celebrate your achievements, consistently work toward your goals, and do not give up when you experience a setback.

Keep up the good work, stay dedicated, and don't surrender even if you hit rock bottom. Always keep going.

II. Mental Health and Stress Management

Stress and anxiety are the usual reactions that take over the body in challenging situations and keep people alive by making them aware of the threat. Indeed, if the stress symptoms persist for longer, the body and mind cannot be resistant and will be significantly undermined by stress. It may differ in how it affects the body – from headaches to sleeping disorders with a reduced immune system.

In this ever-busy world, you should take care of your mental health seriously because your inner peace is paramount, regardless of how many tasks you do. Nevertheless, appreciating mental health awareness and working on stress management will smoothen the way in life and put the stress between more balanced and supportive sides.

Together, let's explore the ways to **manage stress effectively:**

Food Your Body, Nurture Your Brain

First, ensure your body gets the required daily nutrition by leading a balanced diet that fills your body with essential nutrients. Besides physical health, a healthy diet is also of extreme importance to well-being and even to mood.

Embrace Active Living

Regularly, physical activity will act as an antithesis to stress and anxiety. Participate in the things that get your body working, maybe the daily walk or the dance class you have been thinking of. Exercising triggers the secretion of endorphins while creating a euphoric experience, leaving you with an uplifting feeling. Try to include fun stuff in your activities to help you get the most benefits of an active way of living.

Seize an Opportunity to be Calm in a Busy World

Integrate those techniques into your daily relaxations to reduce stress and anxiety. Breathing exercises, meditation, and mindfulness can keep our mind calm, thus shifting it into the zone, which brings us inner peace and calm. Schedule a time slot each day for relaxing and recharging, even if it will be just a few minutes of a deep breath or a quiet meditation.

Prioritize Sleep Hygiene

High-quality sleep is a critical basis for effectively operating body and spirit. Develop a regular sleep pattern and a delightful bedtime ritual to demonstrate to your body that it pleads you to calm down. Ways to create an environment that will promote restful sleep include putting the screens away, creating a comfortable sleeping environment, and adopting relaxation techniques when one cannot sleep because these will help promote sleep.

Foster Positive Thinking

Instead of worrying about the negatives, make a list of the good things you foresee the future bringing. Renounce self-limiting ideas, declare them vacant, and give them empowering optimum thoughts. Nurture thankfulness by realizing the good around you at this particular moment. Also, take time to celebrate your small successes.

Connect with Others

Find your emotional strength from people who love and care about you and perhaps a mental health expert when you begin to struggle with stress or anxiety. Opening up to reliable friends and families relieves you from inner tensions and also gives another thought that could be valid.

Practice Self-Care

Self-care should be a top priority, and you can pursue this by taking simple activities such as meditation, yoga, and your favorite hobbies that feed your mind, body, and spirit. You could do it by walking through nature, choosing to do what interests you, or even enjoying a relaxing bath. Note, too, that taking care of yourself is not selfish at all-it is the key to long-term health and happiness!

Manage Time Wisely

Appropriate time management can avoid the anxiety caused by numerous obligations and assignments. To maintain a balance between work and private life, set priorities among tasks, define realistic goals, and distribute them when needed. Use organizers such as planners and calendars to maintain rhythm while preventing task postponement.

Stay Mindful

Using mindfulness practices, monitor your current moment-to-moment experiences, like thoughts, feelings, and perceptions. Examples of mindfulness meditation, deep breathing exercises, and body scans are some tools that can help you in the moment, help you forget about your problems, stress less, and even make you more.

Practicing these techniques daily allows you to develop resilience and inner strength and gracefully overcome life's challenges. Remember that mental health is your priceless treasure—treat it with gentleness and love!

III. Personal Hygiene and Self-Care

Self-care is concerned with caring for your body and sense of being. It is an act of keeping oneself clean and healthy and being visited by medical personnel when the need arises. Furthermore, it is recommended that methods be used adequately to cope with stressful situations. In a way, self-care involves mainly making your health and general well-being the main priority.

In a study published in 2018, self-care was defined as "the self-initiated behavior that people choose to incorporate to promote good health and general well-being, and something that also encompasses coping strategies to deal with work stress."

Here are some simple self-care ideas:

- Journal
- Practice mindful breathing daily
- Eat breakfast
- Reflect on gratitude each night
- Put your phone on airplane mode before bed
- Call a friend
- Enjoy a relaxing hobby
- Stick to a bedtime routine

These are some Essential Self-Care Practices for Well-being that will help you out in achieving a healthier lifestyle:

1. **Health Literacy:** Comprehending health information is crucial. Check sources, learn to ask questions, and seek help from healthcare professionals.
2. **Mental Wellness:** Make mental health a priority by doing things to reduce stress and by understanding your health problem.
3. **Physical Activity:** Exercising regularly reduces the risk of most health conditions, eases tension, and increases general mental well-being, improving sleep quality.
4. **Balanced Diet:** A nutritious diet promotes health, reduces risks of diseases, and supports normal bodily functions.
5. **Hygiene Habits:** Observe a good hygiene regimen to stay healthy and improve your general health.

Like all forms of self-care, personal hygiene is an essential part. It maintains social and psychological well-being and protects it from loneliness and social isolation. One way of taking care of bodies is by keeping them safe and healthy, ensuring the environment is positive for good health. Here are some simple yet crucial practices to incorporate into your daily routine:

Negative Effects Of Poor Personal Hygiene

- Body lice
- Athlete's foot
- Chronic Diarrhea
- Head lice
- Pinworms
- Ringworm

1. **Shower Regularly:** Regular showering should be your daily habit because it removes sweat and dirt from your body. Make sure you wash these areas with a lot of water to reduce fungal growth.
2. **Hand Washing:** Hand washing with soap or sanitizer is often necessary, especially after using electronic devices or keys. This prevents the transmission of germs and bacteria.
3. **Oral Hygiene:** Fluoridated toothpaste should be used at least twice a day. It helps prevent dental caries (tooth decay) and gum disease. Furthermore, flossing after meals is very helpful in removing plaque and food residues, preventing decay, and purifying the breath.
4. **Nail and Hair Care:** Regularly trimmed nails are preventive measures against the accumulation of dirt that can result in possible food poisoning. Also, wash your hair at least twice a week. This is more effective in removing excess oil and dirt, which is good for a healthy scalp.
5. **Clothing Hygiene:** Change to clean and fresh clothes often to maintain other hygiene and freshness. Provide adequate washing instructions using the correct detergent to eradicate bacteria and microbes.
6. **Food Hygiene:** Ensure safe food handling procedures to prevent food poisoning cases. Make sure meats are thoroughly cooked and contaminated cross-contamination is avoided by washing hands and utensils carefully.

PERSONAL HEALTH AND WELLNESS

7. **Menstrual Hygiene and Genital Hygiene:** Change the pad or tampon frequently, and afterward, gently wipe the genital area with an unscented mild soap and water. Do not use soap inside the vagina to keep the balance of the bacteria in the vagina.
8. **Preventing Body Odor:** Shower often, soap up, and finish with deodorant to add freshness to your body. Wear clothes made from fabrics such as cotton and wash your garments regularly.

IV. Understanding and Navigating Healthcare

Traversing the multifaceted macrocosm of healthcare can be challenging, but having the best health status is necessary. This section will discuss the fundamental elements of healthcare systems and basic healthcare needs.

1. **Healthcare Systems Overview:** Healthcare systems may differ from country to country, but they all aim to give people access to medical services and allow health to thrive. Getting the type of care you require is essential to grasping the intricacies of your community's healthcare system.
2. **Primary Care vs. Specialty Care:** The primary link between the individual and the healthcare system is the primary care provider, such as general practitioners or family doctors. They treat common health problems, offer preventive care services, and refer patients to specialists in case of need.
3. **Health Insurance and Medical Care:** Insurance coverage is one of the major factors in responding to healthcare and provides a vital gateway to healthcare services. Understanding your health insurance plan, consisting of deductibles, coinsurance, and covered services, is vital to your healthcare decisions. Moreover, learning how to work through insurance networks and knowing where in-network providers are can help avoid extra expenses.
4. **Preventive Health Services and Screening:** Prevention encompasses maintaining health and diagnosing diseases early

through routine inspection, vaccination, and lifestyle adjustment. Appreciating well-being and observing timely assessments, including recommended diagnostics, can help locate health issues quickly and improve health results.

5. **Managing Chronic Conditions:** The long-term nature of conditions like diabetes, hypertension, or asthma calls for thorough day-to-day management of the symptoms so that serious complications may be prevented. Adopting personal skills to handle chronic diseases, such as medication management, lifestyle modification, and chronic disease management, is the core of maintaining a good quality of life and decreasing healthcare expenses.

6. **Emergency Care and Urgent Care:** Knowing the distinction between emergency and urgent care is indispensable when dealing with sudden health issues. Emergency departments are designed to deal with life-threatening emergencies like chest pain or severe injuries, unlike urgent care centers, which provide prompt care for non-life-threatening conditions such as minor injuries or infections.

7. **Patient Rights and Advocacy:** As a patient, you have claims related to immediate medical care that must be met, and you also have provisions to honor. Recognition of your rights, like informed consent and privacy, puts you in charge, allowing you to participate actively in the decision-making process about your health.

8. **Telehealth and Digital Health:** Innovations in technology have essentially changed how healthcare services are provided through telehealth and digital health platforms, which provide direct access to medical care. Awareness of the use of telemedicine, such as virtual consultations and remote monitoring, will help people have greater flexibility, control, and convenience in healthcare.

9. **Making Patient-Provider Relationship:** Developing a supportive and trusting relationship with your healthcare provider is key to getting individualized and quality care. Effective communication, mutual appreciation, and shared

decision-making are the main elements of successful interactions between patients and their medical providers. This can result in trust and collaboration toward achieving overall healthiness.

Knowing and using healthcare systems are the main means to meet basic healthcare needs, stay healthy, and get well. Understanding the basics of healthcare, such as insurance, preventive care, and patient rights, will enable you to make informed choices and advocate for your health effectively. Keep in mind that knowledge is power when it comes to dealing with the navigation of healthcare.

Key Takeaways

- Prioritize a balanced diet of fruits, vegetables, whole grains, and lean proteins to promote overall health.
- Engage in regular physical activity.
- Recognize the importance of mental health awareness and stress management in today's fast-paced world.
- Understand the impact of stress on physical and mental well-being and adopt effective strategies to manage stress levels.
- Practice mindfulness, relaxation techniques, and positive thinking to promote mental well-being.
- Embrace self-care as a means of tending to physical and emotional health needs.
- Prioritize practices such as regular hygiene routines, maintaining oral health, and practicing good nutrition habits.
- Familiarize yourself with your local healthcare system, including primary and specialty care services.
- Understand your health insurance coverage and how to navigate insurance networks to minimize out-of-pocket costs.
- Advocate for your health by understanding patient rights, engaging in preventive care, and building a strong patient-provider relationship.

Diet Plan For Young Adults

Here's a structured diet plan for a healthy, balanced diet for young adults, including the recommended amounts of protein, carbohydrates, and other essential nutrients:

Breakfast:

Scrambled eggs with spinach and wholegrain toast.
- *Protein:* 2eggs (12g)
- *Carbohydrates:* Taro and sweet potato are also sources of complex carbohydrates that help to regulate blood sugar levels.
- *Other nutrients:* Spinach has vitamins A, C, and K that a body needs.

Mid-Morning Snack:

Greek yogurt with fresh berries and granola sprinkled on top.
- *Protein:* 1 serving cup of Greek yogurt (15g)
- *Carbohydrates:* 1/2 cup of mixed with berries (10 g) to serve.
- *Other nutrients:* Fiber and healthy fats in granola.

Lunch:

- Grilled chicken salad with mixed baby greens, cherry tomatoes, cucumbers, and sweet balsamic vinaigrette.
- *Protein:* 4 ounces of grilled chicken breast (25 kg)
- *Carbohydrates:* The baby may use various vegetables with fiber and about 15-20g of carbohydrates.
- *Other nutrients:* Healthy fats from the dressing and vegetables.

Afternoon Snack:

- Handful of a combination of mixed nuts (almonds, walnuts, and cashews)
- *Protein:* In general, about 5g of protein.
- *Carbohydrates:* On average, about 5g of carbohydrates.
- *Other nutrients:* Healthy fats, vitamins, and minerals.

Dinner:

- Let the baked salmon be with roasted sweet potatoes and steamed broccoli.
- *Protein:* 4 ounces of salmon (20-25g) are one serving/portion.
- *Carbohydrates:* 1 potato of sweat taste (26g)
- *Other nutrients:* Broccoli provides fiber, vitamins, and minerals.

Evening Snack:

- Plain Greek yogurt with a drizzle of honey and cut-up strawberries
- *Protein:* Per 1 cup Greek yogurt serving (15g).
- *Carbohydrates:* I use only 1/2 a cup of strawberries (6g)
- *Other nutrients:* Honey adds natural richness, sweetness, vitamins, and minerals.

Total Daily Intake:

- *Protein:* Approximately 90-100g
- *Carbohydrates:* Approximately 150-160g
- *Other nutrients:* The content of fiber, healthy fats, vitamins, and minerals from different sources during the day will ensure the body does not miss any of these substances.

Remember to adjust portion sizes based on individual needs and activity levels and consult with a healthcare professional or registered dietitian for personalized dietary recommendations.

CHAPTER 9

Practical Life Skills

CHAPTER 8 BROUGHT about the notion of fitness, but what about your practical life skills? Do not worry. This guide is here to help you! In this chapter, we are going to get practical – diving into those teeny-tiny hacks that keep you on track instead of getting lost in the confusion of teenage life. So, here we go, and let's learn to be a practical teen like a pro!

I. Basic First Aid and Safety Tips

Picture yourself being the one to rush to the rescue when somebody faces a sudden illness or injury. That is the moment when the role of basic first aid is highlighted. From trivial accidents to alarming situations, knowing how to provide first aid can help save lives. Here, we'll discuss the basic definition of first-aid, the role of this practice in saving lives, and its efficacy for quick recovery. In addition, we will talk about what skills are necessary to administer aid as fast as possible. Therefore, let's arm ourselves with the knowledge and confidence to deal with unexpected situations with dignity and competence.

First aid is the first step in treating someone who is injured before medical treatment is available. It focuses on saving a life, preventing deterioration, and encouraging recovery. Fundamental first aid knowledge is sufficient to be useful in cases like incidents at work, at home, or in public. Let's explore some essential tips for handling common medical situations and ensuring readiness and well-being for all.

Checking ABC (Airway, Breathing, Circulation)

First is the assessment of the casualty's airway, breathing, and circulation, often referred to as ABC. Among people without consciousness, clear the airways by freeing their mouths, slightly positioning the head backward, and lifting the chin. This ensures the airway is not blocked, aiding respiration. For those who are breathing but unconscious, place them in a recovery position to keep the airway open and prevent choking on vomit or saliva.

Preventing Bleeding

For profuse bleeding, apply gentle yet firm pressure over the affected area using a clean and dry cloth or dressings to curtail the situation. If possible, elevate the injured limb to reduce blood flow to the area and help stimulate clotting. However, don't raise the limb if you suspect a fracture.

Benefits Of First Aid Knowledge

- Emergency Support
- Personal Awareness
- Life-Saving Procedures
- Promoting Safety
- Confidence to Act

Burns and Scalds

The fast intervention will provide the right treatment for burns and scalds, reducing tissue damage and pain. First, try running cool water on your burn for approximately 10 minutes to dissipate the heat and decrease the pain. Remove all clothes and jewelry near the burn site, but do not apply creams or ointments, as these may worsen the injury.

Sprains

For relief from sprains and strains, the R. I. C. E. method (Rest, Ice, Compression, and Elevation) may provide some consolation and reduce swelling. To reduce the puffiness and inflammation of the region, put an ice pack wrapped in a cloth on the affected area for 15 to 20 minutes, three times an hour.

Diarrhea

In cases of diarrhea, the main thing is to rehydrate to prevent dehydration, which can worsen it. Focus on the person drinking lots of fluids, such as water or electrolyte drinks, to compensate for the deficiency of fluids and salts.

Trauma

Accident-related injuries, such as falls or collisions, must be treated as early as possible to avoid more serious problems. Ask the person to remain still and in the same position to minimize the risk of further injuries, especially spinal trauma.

CPR (Cardiopulmonary Resuscitation)

CPR is a life-saving technique used to maintain blood flow and oxygenation in cardiac arrest or respiratory failure cases. Knowing how to perform CPR correctly is very important. To perform CPR on a person, place the heel of one hand in the center of the chest and interlock both hands, delivering compressions in a rhythmic pattern of 100 to 120 per minute.

Gathering Essential Supplies

Ensure you have access to basic first aid supplies, such as bandages, gauze pads, adhesive tape, antiseptic wipes, scissors, and gloves. A fully stocked first-aid kit can be a valuable tool in helping you handle different medical crises and accidents if they arise.

Seeking Professional Help

First aid can be very effective in emergencies where it provides immediate aid, but such cases often require referral to a doctor for a thorough assessment of the problem. Call emergency services quickly, briefly inform them about the type of emergency, and let them know the person's condition.

We all should be well-prepared for emergencies. Acquiring and cultivating emergency first aid and safety skills will make you competent enough to offer immediate help when needed.

II. Cooking and Meal Preparation

Are you fed up with spending hours in the kitchen every day, but your only choice is what to cook? Fear not! Welcome to meal prepping, a game-changer in home cooking.

But first, you must know what meal prepping is.

Meal prepping is one strategy that can help you avoid fast food. It lasts 3 to 7 days, a method that helps ease the cooking task every night. It means you are making your meals and dividing them into portions to make convenient, "grab-and-go" options for later. No matter the case, it could be packing leftovers for lunch or recipe prep; it will soon be realized that this lifestyle is all about stress-free and efficient eating.

It saves time on busy weeknights, reduces food waste, reduces the temptation to eat out impulsively, and promotes healthier eating habits. Let's talk about some easy-to-go cooking and meal-prepping techniques:

Step 1: Determine the Best Prep Method

Make-ahead meals: This type of meal is great for those with a tight schedule since it means prepping the whole dish and heating it up when you are ready to eat.

Batch cooking/freezing: Make some tasty side dishes and portion them out to save for later.

Individually portioned meals: Make individual servings by dividing the food into smaller portions for on-the-go meals.

Ready-to-cook ingredients: Preparing ingredients ahead of time will make handling the strain of cooking weeknight dinners easier when pressed for time.

Step 2: Devise your Plan

The last thing you want to do is eat the same meal for the whole month. Choosing a meal that will fit you best according to your schedule and preferences is better. Write out your weekly menu, including tried-and-true dishes and one or two new recipes you would like to introduce into the rotation.

Step 3: Shop and Stock

Pre-storing your pantry items and fridge necessities will make eating prep as easy as pie. Compile a complete list logically for time-efficient grocery shopping according to each department. Remember to have different storage containers for the prepped ingredients and meals.

Step 4: Prep and Store

Try to begin cooking with the foods that need the longest cooking time and ensure you always maximize your efficiency. Be aware of your prepped ingredients and storage life, and store the food correctly to ensure their freshness as you plan your meals in advance. Freeze meals correctly to maintain their best quality, labeling and dating the containers for easy reference.

Step 5: Enjoy the Fruits of Your Effort

As you practice, find a suitable meal prep routine—either prep ingredients for one meal or an entire week. Start enjoying the convenience and benefits of meal prepping, which can range from saving time and money to having a healthier and less stressful way of eating.

With the help of basic cooking techniques and the meal preparation tips provided here, even beginners can beat the kitchen chaos and taste the sweetness of home-cooked meals, which are delicious and not stressful. Grab your silverware and apron to kick start the fun and tasty meal prep session!

Essential Food Equipment:

- Food Processor
- Chopper
- Slicer
- Grill
- Oven
- Toaster
- Rolling pin
- Baking sheet
- Steamer
- Deep fryer

III. Basic Home Maintenance and Repair

Have you ever seen cottages built several centuries ago with full architectural details still intact? We are about to uncover the mystery of home maintenance and repair, where just a pinch of DIY tricks can transform the entire picture.

Maintaining and repairing your home is a regular duty to which you should be committed. Whenever problems arise, you should be the first one to fix them. It is like taking a health check of your home to make sure that it remains in the best condition. Therefore, get yourself set to face the learning curve of doing your own home maintenance and repairs!

1. **Schedule Your Maintenance:** Make a thorough maintenance plan to organize the entire affair and ensure that objects like gutter cleaning, air filter replacement, smoke detector inspection, and so on are attended to regularly. You can use calendars or spreadsheets to schedule maintenance tasks and set reminders for usual checks and replacements.

2. **Examine Your Roof:** You should check your roof frequently for signs of damage, including breakage or misplaced tiles, cracked sealant, or sagging areas. To avoid this problem, you may hire a professional roofing contractor to do an annual inspection to detect potential problems initially.

3. **Clean Gutters and Downspouts:** Avoid water damage and foundation issues by making sure your gutters and downspouts are free from debris and given regular cleaning. Pick a strong step ladder and wear gloves to clean up leaves, twigs, and other obstacles so they won't block the path of rainwater away from your house.

4. **Examine Your Doors and Windows:** Seal all doors, windows, and other openings with loose weather stripping or other imperfections that could diminish the building's energy efficiency. Additionally, you may need to change the seals and put them on the weather strip to boost insulation and cut bills.

> **Links to DIY Home Repair Videos:**
>
> **Fixing a Leaky Faucet:** DIY Faucet Repair
> **Unclogging a Drain:** DIY Drain Unclogging
> **Repairing Drywall Holes:** DIY Drywall Repair
> **Replacing a Broken Tile:** DIY Tile Replacement
> **Fixing a Running Toilet:** DIY Toilet Repair

5. **Clean or Replace a Faucet Aerator:** The water flow and pressure restoration can be achieved by cleaning or replacing the aerator, which can get clogged with mineral deposits over time. Disassemble the aerator and soak it in vinegar to break down residues. After this, thoroughly clean it with a brush and tighten it back or replace it with a new one (if necessary).
6. **Replace Air Filters:** Sustain healthy indoor air quality and efficiency of the heating, ventilation, and air conditioning system by changing air filters every 30 days or as recommended by the manufacturer. Be sure to pick high-quality filters with a MERV rating that is just right for your system to trap dust, pollen, and other airborne particles effectively.

Regularly performing these basic maintenance tasks can help you maintain your house in optimal condition and make your life easier by reducing time, cost, and stress in the future.

IV. Managing Personal Documentation

Managing personal documents may appear tiresome, but the right devices and methods will turn a mess into order efficiently and save you time and effort in the future. Picture never again struggling to locate that important document or wasting time looking through heaps of papers. With just a few easy hacks, you can make organizing simple and ensure that the paperwork you need can easily be located.

Let's consider some tips for handling and organizing personal documents systematically.

1. **Separate Documents by Type:** First, identify the different categories and subcategories of documents. For example, reports, documents, quotes, assignments, and billing invoices can be sorted into distinct categories to make it easier to find desirable paperwork when needed.
2. **Use Chronological and Alphabetical Order:** After you have put all documents in order, consider time-stamping them. For example, sorting the documents from newest to oldest makes it easy to find the latest information. Furthermore, documents can be placed alphabetically by name or form.

> **The Most Important Documents to Keep:**
>
> - Social Security Cards
> - Birth Certificates
> - Legal Identification Documents
> - Marriage Certificates
> - Passports
> - Tax Documents
> - Property Records
> - Life Insurance Policies
> - Medical Bills
> - Financial Records
> - Vehicle Registration and Titles
> - Investment Statements

3. **Organize Your Filing Space:** Make use of file cabinets and drawers to arrange your documents systematically. Files folded are really good when classifying and subgrouping your documents according to the document type. Also, file shelves have a purpose when they involve files and documents you use frequently.
4. **Color-Code Your Filing System:** Visual markers like colored tabs can simplify finding the required document. Sorting various document colors into different folders makes it easier to find important papers in a snap of a finger.

5. **Label Your Filing System:** Labeling documents is important for credibility, usefulness, and organization. Employ label makers or colored pens to make labels for folders, shelves, or cabinets.
6. **Dispose of Unnecessary Documents:** De-clutter by sorting the documents you normally need from the ones you don't. Recycling or shredding obsolete documents cuts down the chaos and mitigates the security and compliance risks in your workplace.
7. **Digitize Files:** Think about going digital so you can increase accessibility and reduce the amount of clutter. Scan the paperwork into digital files and arrange them in sections on your computer. Establish a routine pattern, similar to a physical filing, by applying the sorting, organizing, color-coding, and labeling techniques for digital documents to make them easy to describe.

Effective management of personal documents is the main factor for an orderly and stress-free environment. Applying these real-life approaches, you can turn your paperwork into a well-organized system that promotes productivity and relaxes your mind.

To make the organizational process more efficient, gather the following items:

- Durable binders and dividers
- Sheet protectors for dividing documents
- Labels and labeling stickers for categorization
- Document sleeves for protection
- Sticky notes for differentiation
- Medium-size boxes to prevent damage.

Key Takeaways

- Learn CPR and basic first aid techniques.
- Keep a first aid kit readily accessible.
- Be aware of potential hazards and take preventive measures.
- Embrace meal prepping for convenience and efficiency.
- Choose a meal prep method that suits your schedule.
- Plan meals to save time and money.
- Utilize basic cooking techniques and simple recipes.
- Maintain a well-organized kitchen for easier meal prep.
- Regularly maintain and repair your home to save money in the long run.
- Conduct routine inspections of key areas like the roof and gutters.
- Clean appliances and systems to ensure proper functionality.
- Keep important documents like IDs, certificates, and financial records safe.
- Use organizational tools like binders, folders, and labels.
- Sort documents by type and subtype for easy categorization.
- Consider digitizing files for accessibility and reduced clutter.

Exercise

Home Maintenance and Repair Checklist

1. Inspect Roof:

[ ] Inspect the roof for damage.
[ ] Replace damaged or missing shingles.

2. Clean Gutters and Downspouts:

[ ] Clean out gutters and downspouts.
[ ] Ensure proper drainage away from the house.

3. Clean or Replace a Faucet Aerator:

[ ] Clean Faucet Aerator monthly.
[ ] Replace them annually.

4. Inspect Doors and Windows:

[ ] Check for drafts around doors and windows.
[ ] Replace weather stripping if necessary.

5. Clean or Replace Air Filters:

[ ] Replace air filters every 30 days.
[ ] Clean ground-level return air vents.

6. Inspect Plumbing:

[ ] Check for leaks under sinks and around toilets.
[ ] Repair any leaks promptly.

7. Inspect HVAC System:

[ ] Schedule annual maintenance for heating and cooling systems.
[ ] Change air filters regularly.

8. DIY Repair Practice:

[ ] Watch DIY repair videos for hands-on learning.
[ ] Practice basic repairs under supervision.

CHAPTER 10

Preparing for the Future

"By failing to prepare, you are preparing to fail."
— **Benjamin Franklin**

RECALL YOUR LIFE as a book with new pages to read every day. The pages ahead are bare, without a word of your narrative. How are you going to mold your tomorrow? In this chapter, we will delve into how to come up with achievable goals, setting plans for short-term and long-term goals, the evolutionary phenomenon of change and adaptability, the necessity of life-long learning, and the way in which we eventually create our own path to success. Let's start figuring out the ways that will prepare you for what lies ahead!

Setting Long-Term and Short-Term Goals

Imagine your life as a journey, with each goal you set acting as a milestone on the path to your destination. Goal setting is the process of identifying what you want to achieve and mapping out the steps to get there. It's a powerful tool for bringing about positive change in your life.

Goals can be divided into two broad categories: short-term goals and long-term goals.

Difference Between Short-Term and Long-Term Goals

Aspect	Short-Term Goals	Long-Term Goals
Time	Achievable within weeks or months	Takes several years to achieve
Strategy	Focus on immediate action and tactics	Requires planning, persistence, and strategic approach
Motivation	Provides quick results for immediate motivation.	Feels distant; gives direction and purpose
Flexibility	Needs hard deadlines for progress	Benefits from flexibility and adjustments
Multitask	Easily manageable and allows multitasking	Several short-term goals can support them

I. Short-Term Goals

Short-term goals are the immediate objectives you aim to achieve within a short period, usually within weeks, months, or up to one year. These goals are specific, actionable, and designed to guide you toward quick progress. Setting short-term goals can be a powerful way to make consistent progress toward your bigger dreams. Below are three key steps to help you plan and achieve your short-term goals effectively.

1. Identify Long-Term Goals

Understanding your long-term goals is crucial because it allows you to break them down into smaller, manageable tasks. Think about a significant goal that will take time and effort to achieve, such as starting your own business or completing a degree. By knowing where you ultimately want to go, you can create short-term goals that act as stepping stones toward that bigger objective.

2. Set SMART Goals

The SMART formula is an optimal tool to assist you in the achievement of your objectives more effectively by consolidating them and enabling you to do so. The SMART criteria ensure that your goals are:
   a. **Specific:** More specifically, state what you want to achieve.
   b. **Measurable:** Ensure you are monitoring your progress closely.
   c. **Achievable:** Establish achievable yet significant goals that stimulate you to do your best.
   d. **Relevant:** Ensure that your goals are in line with your long-term goals and values.
   e. **Time-based:** Establish a deadline and use it to motivate and keep you attainable.

For example, a SMART goal could be: "In the next 30 days, I will shape a new marketing set-up for my business. "

3. Take Note of Your Own Progress

The most important aspect is to control your actions regularly to keep you motivated and stay on track. Here are some practical ways to track your short-term goals:
   a. **Journal Your Progress:** Do daily entries about what complete tasks you have done toward your goal.
   b. **Use a Tally System:** Remember to add records of the number of days you have been working on your goals.
   c. **Accountability Partner:** A mentor or a close friend can be your helpdesk in holding you accountable, and in doing so, you can share your goals and progress with them.
   d. **Visualization:** Spend a couple of hours imagining reaching your aim every day. This can be very motivational.

By doing so, you can develop and achieve short-term goals that lead to your long-term dreams.

II. Long-Term Goals

In contrast, long-term goals are the broader visions that you have about your future that typically last for many years. These goals are more comprehensive and less detailed than short-term goals. Patience, persistence, and strategic planning are some of the things that are necessary for achieving long-term goals. Here are some methods to help you envision and reach your long-term aspirations:

1. Envision Your Future

Consider where you will be in 10 years. It includes financial, personal, and career goals and different categories like these. By ensuring that your objectives go hand-in-hand with what is significant or close to you, you give them more meaning and become more focused on achieving them.

2. Work Backwards from Your Goal

Start at the finish line as though you were already at your goal. With this method, you follow the steps one by one so that the process feels less overwhelming. Visualizing your achievements can give you extra insights and motivation about how to reach your goal.

3. Break Them into Small and Achievable Goals

Divide your long-term goals into smaller and manageable tasks. For example, if your long-term objective is to write a novel, set yourself a short-term target of 100 words per day. This can be accomplished by setting small attainable goals, which are all part of achieving the final goals.

> **Benefits of Setting Long-term Goals**
>
> **Clarity and Direction:** Long-term goals provide clear focus and direction.
>
> **Increased Motivation:** Working toward a long-term goal is highly motivating and gives a sense of purpose.
>
> **Greater Achievement:** Achieving a long-term goal feels more rewarding than short-term goals.
>
> **Improved Decision-making:** Long-term goals help prioritize time and resources effectively.
>
> **Personal Growth:** Pursuing long-term goals fosters personal growth and overall well-being.

4. Set Monthly Short-Term Goals

Write down your list of goals after a monthly review and set new short-term goals based on your current life situation. This consistent check-in helps you stay on track and allows you to adapt your plan accordingly.

5. Be Flexible with Goals as Plans Change

Life is dynamic, and a goal you are pursuing heavily can soon become less important while another goal finds its way into your priorities. Make sure you check with yourself and are open and flexible about any changes, adjustments, or even replacements of the originally planned activities.

Both short- and long-term goals are essential for success. Achieving short-term goals helps build momentum and confidence, paving the way for tackling more significant, long-term goals. Remember, each step you take brings you closer to your ultimate dreams.

III. Embracing Change and Adaptability

Dean Becker, a well-known resilience expert, notes that adaptability is the foundation of survival in all spheres of life. According to him, achievements aren't purely tied to education, intellect, or experience. Thus, ultimately, it's our flexibility that really makes a difference. Whether it's sports, medicine, business, or anything else, after all, it is the adaptable people who survive and prosper.

Adopting change and adaptability is not just about being flexible; it is even more than that; it is about surviving a world where change is the only constant. Now, it is time to discuss the significance of adaptability in both personal and professional life.

1. Increased Workplace Value

It is no doubt that adaptability is the most wanted skill in contemporary business. Employers seek workers who are adaptable and innovative and drive changes to create growth for the companies. Applying adaptability skills enables individuals like you to increase their marketability and hold on to the competition in the highly governed job market.

2. Essential Leadership Skill

Effective leaders must be flexible to deal with the mentioned obstacles and uncertainties. Change-embracing leaders not only lead their teams but also create resilience and navigate the way to success for their organizations, even during times of instability.

3. Enhanced Happiness and Life Satisfaction

Adaptability leads to the development of resilience, and as a result, individuals can overcome setbacks and achieve happiness even when facing challenges. By managing change and learning from failures, one can experience a more complete and comfortable life.

4. Smooth Career Transitions

Because the career market is fairly dynamic, adaptability becomes a necessity and the proper tool for facing career changes and transitions. Adaptable individuals can expand their horizons, pick up a wide range of skills, and perform well in various jobs, increasing their chances for success.

5. Resilience in Adversity

Life is unpredictable, and adaptability assists in coping with and recovering from failures. Although not flexible when it comes to overcoming challenges, adaptable individuals embrace change and grow beyond these problems.

Adaptability is an important prerequisite for success in the modern world, which is constantly changing. Cultivating change through the embracement of adaptability can help in this endeavor. Hence, individuals like you, whether leaders or employees, will become more valuable, will find their personal happiness, and can thrive at work or after losing a job. Adaptability is one of the key skills of personal growth, professional progress, and psychological health.

How to Develop an Adaptable Mindset

1. **Embrace Change:** Accept that change is constant and welcome it.
2. **Stay Curious:** Seek new information and perspectives to stay ahead.
3. **Be Open-minded:** Be receptive to new ideas and approaches.
4. **Embrace Failure:** View failure as a learning opportunity.
5. **Encourage Experimentation:** Foster a culture where trying new things is encouraged.

IV. Continuous Learning and Self-Improvement

"Continuous learning and self-improvement are the keystones to unlocking our fullest potential, guiding us toward a future defined by growth and achievement."

— John Doe

Continuous or life-long learning is always in the process of individual and professional development, which is necessary to cope with the manifestations of our ever-changing world. Today, we are in a world where lifetime learning and continuous self-improvement are indispensable parts of personal and professional development. It could be arguably thought that there are innumerable benefits to continuous learning. Let us go deeper into the importance of lifelong learning and self-improvement in dealing with complex issues in this dynamic environment.

1. Improve Personal and Professional Skills

Having active involvement in lifelong learning broadens our knowledge. It enhances skills like problem-solving, creativity, and adaptability, which, as a result, give zest to our lives as individuals and professionals.

2. Unleashing Potential

Lifelong learning and continuous self-improvement are a pair of dynamic duos that help people find their unexplored talents. Constant learning and personal development could help people discover fresh interests, refine existing skills, and open up chances for progress.

3. Fueling Innovation

Lifelong learning is the driving force for innovation and dwells on the virtues of imagination, curiosity, and audacity. While people pursue their personal development, they add fresh ideas, new viewpoints, and game-changing solutions to the world.

4. Empowering Careers

Lifelong learning and continuous self-improvement become a springboard for further career promotion and professional success. Through engaging in constant learning, expanding one's competency areas, and adapting to the emerging trends in the industry, such individuals will be able to boost their careers to the most incredible heights and fulfill their dreams.

Examples of Lifelong Learning

1. Developing New Skills: Sewing, cooking, programming, public speaking, etc.

2. Self-Taught Study: Learning a new language, researching topics of interest, and subscribing to podcasts.

3. Learning New Sports or Activities: Martial arts, skiing, exercise routines.

4. Mastering New Technologies: Smart devices, software applications.

5. Acquiring New Knowledge: Online courses, classroom-based courses.

5. Enhancing Well-being:

Profitable growth, lifelong learning, and steady self-improvement will stimulate profound personal development. Developing meaningful learning experiences, following a personal passion, and mastering practical life skills all lead to greater satisfaction, resilience, and, ultimately, life enjoyment.

In the end, the process of lifelong learning and continuous self-improvement is not just a goal. It is a transitional journey that enriches lives, empowers individuals like you, and lays a foundation for the better-coming generation.

V. The Path to Personal and Professional Success

After discussing the importance of lifelong learning and constant self-improvement, it's time to embark on a journey of personal and professional progression. Let's look at an exciting aspect that always catches people's attention: personal and professional development.

Personal Development

Personal development is set through enhancing emotional intelligence, resilience, core values correspondence, and self-actualization. Such an experience is about realizing your biggest potential beyond professional growth. Let me tell you some strategies to head on the path of personal development:

1. **Set Clear Goals:** Develop a strategic and clear-cut plan with objectives that align with your values. Having clear goals that explain what you want and why you want it provides direction and motivation for your personal development.
2. **Continuous Self-Reflection:** It is crucial to consider the strengths and weaknesses you discover about yourself and then try to find places or ways to cultivate those strengths or work on

those weaknesses. Self-awareness is one of the evidence-based techniques aimed at facilitating self-development. It focuses on pinpointing your areas of strength and weakness and on celebrating your achievements.
3. **Embrace Challenges:** Consider challenges to develop yourself rather than treat them as hurdles on your path. Being driven by challenges makes you more resilient and allows you to learn new skills and transcend limitations.
4. **Seek Feedback:** You can gain a fresh perspective by asking for help from mentors, peers, and people with lots of real-life experience. The constructive feedback you receive provides you with insights and perspectives and helps you improve your skills and behaviors.
5. **Practice Self-Care:** Self-care should be a top priority to maintain physical, psychological, and emotional well-being. Get enough sleep, eat well, exercise, and spend some time doing the activities you find rejuvenating to remain active.

Through these strategies becoming part of your routine, your road toward personal achievement and satisfaction is paved.

Professional Development

On the other hand, personal development is intended for both skill honing and knowledge development, and it includes workshops and certification, career progress through the organization, and even climbing the corporate ladder. It is not simply getting prepared for a job but having the guts and determination to flourish and excel in doing well despite the presence of competition in that professional environment.

DID YOU KNOW?

Did you know that networking plays a crucial role in professional success? Studies have shown that up to 85% of jobs are filled through networking, highlighting the importance of building and maintaining professional relationships.

1. **Define Your Career Vision:** Define your career goals and ambitions for the future. Identify areas of employment, job profiles, and occupational environments that best suit your interests, values, and abilities.
2. **Develop Marketable Skills:** Take frequent classes in your niche to upgrade your abilities and knowledge. Seek formal education, certifications, workshops, or some work experience to be relevant and update yourself with the ongoing trends in the job market.
3. **Network Effectively:** Construct and cultivate personal and business contacts among professionals in and outside your field. Engage in networking activities, join different associations, and utilize online connectivity tools to connect with contemporaries, mentors, and future employers.
4. **Seek Growth Opportunities:** Be proactive in looking for opportunities within your current work or use them to advance or even start something new. Participate in difficult projects wisely, take part in leadership positions, and seek opportunities for growth, enhancement, and career advancement.
5. **Stay Constant and Adapt:** Keep up with industry innovations, developments, and changes. Adapt to changing technologies, research methods, and best practices to make sure you stay relevant and competitive in your field.
6. **Demonstrate Leadership Skills:** Discover leadership traits, develop your communication, problem-solving, and decision-making skills, and become a great team player.
7. **Manage Your Personal Brand:** Establish a personal brand that stresses what you believe in, your knowledge, and who you are

as a professional. Build a well-known and organized internet profile. Demonstrate your personal brand through your social media platforms. Illustrate what you have done so far and what your contributions are.

Using these strategies, you can build a platform to achieve professional success and fulfill your career aspirations with confidence and determination.

So now, here you are at the end of the last chapter of this guide, and you are equipped with almost every skill essential for living. Quickly jump to the conclusion to have a list of all the content covered in this book.

Key Takeaways

- Short-term Goals are achievable within weeks or months, helping you make immediate progress and serve as steps toward bigger ambitions.
- Long-term Goals are broader objectives to achieve over the years, requiring planning and patience, often broken down into smaller short-term goals.
- Adaptability means being flexible and resilient in the face of change, allowing you to adjust quickly to new situations and challenges.
- Continuous Learning is the ongoing acquisition of knowledge and skills, crucial for staying relevant in a changing world.
- Self-improvement is personal growth through new perspectives, confidence-building, and enhancing skills like creativity and critical thinking.
- Personal Development focuses on holistic growth, including emotional intelligence and resilience, aiming for fulfillment beyond career goals.
- Professional Development concentrates on career-specific skills and knowledge, aiming for advancement through networking,

staying current with industry trends, and demonstrating leadership abilities.

Exercise: 'Statements and Reasons'

For each statement, write down whether you agree or disagree and provide a reason for your response. Reflect on how these principles apply to your own life and future plans.

Statement 1: Setting short-term goals is more important than setting long-term goals.
Reason: I disagree because both short-term and long-term goals are equally important. Short-term goals provide immediate motivation and progress, while long-term goals give direction and purpose.

Statement 2: Embracing change is essential for personal growth.
Reason:

_____
_____

Statement 3: Continuous learning should be a lifelong commitment.
Reason:

_____
_____

Statement 4: Personal development is as important as professional development.
Reason:

_____
_____

Statement 5: Adapting to new situations quickly is a crucial skill for success in the modern world.
Reason:

_____
_____

Statement 6: Long-term goals require more patience and strategic planning compared to short-term goals.
Reason:

Statement 7: Self-improvement can significantly boost self-confidence and personal fulfillment.
Reason:

Statement 8: Professional development is solely about acquiring new technical skills.
Reason:

Statement 9: Building resilience is crucial in overcoming life's challenges and setbacks.
Reason:

Statement 10: Networking and staying updated with industry trends are vital for career advancement.
Reason:

CONCLUSION

AS YOU STAND on the brink of adulthood, consider this: you not only acquire valuable personal achievements but also learn how to serve the communities. Picture the ripple effect of your choices: the financial smartness you have can motivate other people to become responsible with their finances, the communication skills you have can help in uniting fractured communities, and the problem-solving skills you have can drive innovation and effect change.

Think about the role of small, cumulative efforts. Each choice you make, and each hurdle you leap is part of the web of your life. Whenever you help your friend with their resume, fix a leaky faucet at home, or be organized in your time management, you are improving your life and setting an example for others.

Take a minute to imagine what you want to leave behind as your legacy. How are you going to help the world with your skills and the knowledge you have gained from your education? What is the perspective necessary to learn throughout life and to motivate others to develop as well? The trip does not end now; it is the start of a long journey that will enrich you with transformation, learning, and contribution. Holding this guide will help you take over the world!

It has been a comprehensive journey, a complete guide packed with skills that a teen like you would need as they maneuver through the intricacies of adulthood. The book, divided into 10 chapters, imparted valuable information, approachable strategies, and compelling suggestions on various vital issues. Let's recap if you got it all.

Chapter 1 of this guide focused on mastering money management and discussed how to grasp personal finance, implement plans within budgeting, apply prudent saving to safeguard against future setbacks, evade debt, and use good credit management.

Chapter 2 covered the fundamentals of the job market, such as identifying strengths and interests, putting together an eye-catching resume and cover letter, using job search techniques, and conducting an interview.

Chapter 3 discussed verbal and nonverbal communication, listening and using empathy, overcoming communication barriers, and mastering digital communication.

Chapter 4 discussed different types of relationships, the value of trust and respect, and how to handle conflicts and develop healthy interactions.

Chapter 5 was about developing social skills. It focused on networking, socializing in different settings, online etiquette, and overcoming shyness and social anxiety.

Chapter 6 highlighted various valuable ways to organize time, focus on priorities, overcome procrastination, develop effective studying and working strategies, and achieve harmony between school, work, and private life.

Chapter 7 examined problem identification, analysis, and complexity. It also explained strategic thinking, creativity, and the improvements from mistakes.

Chapter 8 delved into personal health and wellness, serving as a comprehensive guide to nutrition and exercise, mental health and stress management, personal hygiene and self-care, as well as health care navigation.

Chapter 9 discussed first aid and safety, cooking and meal planning, home repairs and maintenance, etc.

Chapter 10 highlighted the importance of setting short-term and long-term goals, developing a growth mindset, nonstop learning, and eventually experiencing personal and professional success.

In sum, this book is a helping guide for teenagers and will help them build a strong and healthy foundation for adulthood. Every chapter has a critical skill necessary for personal development and independence. This guide will also help you grasp crucial matters such as money management, job market searching, effective communication and social skills, time management, critical problem-solving, personal health and maintenance, and other practical tasks in life.

You need to understand that the journey to becoming a capable and confident person takes many paths. Accordingly, it is a blend of essential attributes, such as money smartness, job preparation, effective communication, people management, cooperation, problem-solving, personal health improvement, and practical life skills. Learning these aspects will equip you to address the immediate obstacles and provide a platform for achievement and satisfaction throughout your life.

Be aware because every move you make culminates in realizing and achieving your potential. Follow this guide as you walk your own path to attaining self-reliance, self-awareness, and capability.

Lastly, if you find this guide helpful, I would appreciate your review on Amazon. Your feedback is so important as it will help more people uncover the value of becoming mature individuals. Your review can create confidence and encourage other teenagers to step out of their comfort zones and step on the path of success. Thank you for participating in this discussion and sharing your thoughts and experiences!

Make a Difference with Your Review Personal Finance For Teens

Now you have everything you need to achieve financial success, it's time to pass on your newfound knowledge and show other readers where they can find the same help.

By leaving your honest opinion of this book on Amazon, you'll show other teens where they can find the information they're looking for and pass on your passion for life-long development and success.

Thank you for passing on this life-altering knowledge to help others thrive personally and professionally.

https://www.amazon.com/review/review-your-purchases/?asin=BOOKASIN\

>> Click here to leave your review on Amazon.

ABOUT THE AUTHOR

EMMA DAVIS is a woman who wears many hats. She is a clinical social worker, a therapist, and a financial advisor, as well as the author of Effective Anger Management for Teens.

Her books are aimed at teenagers, covering a diverse range of topics, including life and coping skills, DBT techniques, finances, puberty, developing a growth mindset, and career planning. She focuses on the unique challenges faced by adolescents in their emotional and physiological development, empowering readers with a strong foundation for understanding.

Emma draws on experience and knowledge from all her roles, as well as her experience as a mother, to guide young people through the difficult stage of adolescence. She runs a therapy practice and financial education agency tailored to teenagers, and has worked with a diverse range of young people facing different practical and emotional challenges. She also runs several online courses on cultivating interpersonal skills, gratitude, happiness, and joy, as well as 10 residential care facilities for adults with disabilities and mental health challenges, which also informs her work.

Emma is married with 9 children between the ages of 3 and 22. She enjoys spending time with her family, practicing jiu jitsu, and developing her skills in photography.

Helping Teens With Finances, Anger Management, Mental Health, And Future Life Planning

From

EMMA DAVIS

Available on Amazon or wherever books are sold

To learn more about helping teens with finances, anger management, mental health, and future life planning please join my newsletter! at www.emmadavisbooks.com

REFERENCES

Admin. (2023, March 6). 15 Proven tips to stick to a healthy diet and exercise routine. Docsurgentcare. https://docsmedicalgroup.com/docsurgentcare/15-proven-tips-to-stick-to-a-healthy-diet-and-exercise-routine/

Ahuja, V. (2022, February 10). 7 Ways to Increase Productivity While Studying | HomeGuru. HomeGuru - Connecting Learner to Tutors. https://homeguruworld.com/7-ways-to-increase-productivity-while-studying/

Bartlett MJ, Arslan FN, Bankston A, Sarabipour S. Ten simple rules to improve academic work-life balance. PLoS Comput Biol. 2021 Jul 15;17(7):e1009124. doi: 10.1371/journal.pcbi.1009124. PMID: 34264932; PMCID: PMC8282063.

Bögels, S. (n.d.). Mindfulness-Based Therapy for Social Anxiety Disorder. ResearchGate Logo. https://www.researchgate.net/publication/263443146_Mindfulness-Based_Therapy_for_Social_Anxiety_Disorder

Federal Reserve Board (n.d.). Economic Well-Being of U.S. Households in 2022. Www.federalreserve.gov. https://www.federalreserve.gov/publications/files/2022-report-economic-well-being-us-households-202305.pdf

Managing stress and Anxiety: practical tips and techniques. (2023, June 9). https://www.cathedralcounseling.org/managing-stress-and-anxiety-practical-tips-and-techniques

Mindtools Content Team. (2023). Are You a Procrastinator? Www. mindtools.com. https://www.mindtools.com/agqsnqe/are-you-a-procrastinator

Practical Risk Training. (2021, January 16). Making decisions under uncertainty and risk - Practical Risk Training. https://practicalrisktraining.com/making-decisions-under-uncertainty-and-risk

Rdn, C. H. M. (2021, July 10). A Beginner's Guide to Meal Prep. EatingWell. https://www.eatingwell.com/article/290651/a-beginners-guide-to-meal-prep/

Reesor, S., & Reesor, S. (2020, November 5). 6 basic first aid tips for the workplace. Centre for Security Training & Management Inc. https://www.centreforsecurity.com/6-basic-first-aid-tips-for-the-workplace/

Stevens, A. D. (n.d.). Social problem -solving and cognitive flexibility: Relations to social skills and problem behavior of at -risk young children. ProQuest. https://www.proquest.com/openview/075b0fee377612716a7bf2d352110ac5/1?pq-origsite=gscholar&cbl=18750

Talbert, M. (2022, July 18). How to prioritize your most important work. Asana. https://asana.com/resources/how-prioritize-tasks-work

Witt, R. (n.d.). 4 Ways to Manage and Protect Your Personal Documents - ALCOVA Mortgage. ALCOVA Mortgage. https://alcova.com/4-ways-to-manage-and-protect-your-personal-documents/

Made in the USA
Coppell, TX
18 January 2025

44545083R00085